New Lines of Alliance, New Spaces of Liberty

Félix Guattari & Antonio Negri

Minor Compositions
Autonomedia
MayFlyBooks

Copyright @ 2010 Autonomedia

Main text originally published in French in 1985 as *Les nouveaux espaces de liberté*. First English edition, 1990, published under the title *Communists Like U*s.

ISBN 978-1-57027-224-0
ebook ISBN: 978-1-906948-12-2

Special thanks to Mitch Verter, Arianna Bove, and Matteo Mandarini.

Translated by Michael Ryan, Jared Becker, Arianna Bove, and Noe Le Blanc
Edited by Stevphen Shukaitis.

Released by Minor Compositions, London / New York
Website: www.minorcompositions.info
E-mail: info@minorcompositions.info

Autonomedia
PO Box 568 Williamsburgh Station
Brooklyn, NY 11211-0568 USA
Website: www.autonomedia.org
E-mail: info@autonomedia.org

Published in conjunction with MayFlyBooks.
Website: www.mayflybooks.org.
E-mail: editors@mayflybooks.org

New Lines of Alliance

New Spaces of Liberty

Table of Contents

Introduction: Organising Communism
    Matteo Mandarini   7

1. Communists Like Us   26
2. The Revolution Began in 1968   33
    I. Socialized Production
    II. Beyond Politics
    III. The New Subjectivities
3. The Reaction of the 1970s: No Future   48
    I. Integrated World Capitalism
    II. North/South: Terror and Hunger
    III. The Right in Power
4. The Revolution Continues   63
    I. Recomposition of the Movement
    II. The Terrorist Interlude
5. The New Alliance   77
    I. Molecular Method of Aggregation
    II. Machines on Struggle
    III. Today, New Lines of Alliance
6. Think and Live in Another Way   92

Postscript, 1990
    Antonio Negri   102
Appendix One: The New Spaces of Freedom
    Félix Guattari   116
Appendix Two: Archeological letter. October 1984
    Antonio Negri   128

Organising Communism
Matteo Mandarini[1]

It is said that in the days of the first World War, Vladmir Illic Lenin and Tristan Tzara frequented the same bar in Zurich, without ever encountering one another.

The words of the former wanted to make the world with the strength of the will, the law and of power.

The later enunciated words with irony, as the creation of worlds in which the will, the law and power are suspended.

Had they understood one another, the 1900s would have been much lighter.

Had they been friends they would have constructed spaceships capable of navigating upon the ocean of chaos: rafts for all the refugees that depart [*si allontanano*] from the bellicose and arid lands of late-modern capitalism. – Franco Berardi (*Felix*, p. 140)

This vision of the poet and militant meeting in a small oasis of peace surrounded by war and defeat – the defeat of anti-chauvinist social-democracy – as a moment that could have turned creation into a political weapon and steely will into an open process of collective singularisation, is merely that: an hallucination of a different history.

The encounter of Félix Guattari and Antonio Negri took place in 1977. It was a meeting that occurred in the heat of a battle that no one knew had already been lost, and the result of their collaboration was published in a – comparative – oasis, at least for Negri who had fled Italy for Paris, once the defeat was clear for all to see.

Of course, Negri is not Lenin and Guattari is not Tzara – the *approchement* is no doubt unfair to both, for different reasons. In the one case, it is too much to live up to and, at the same time, reduces the life of a political theorist and philosopher to his militancy; in the other, creativity and poetry can in no way sum up a contribution that spanned the fields of psychiatry, philosophy, semiotics and militant organising. But perhaps this is as close as we have got to such an encounter – for what Franco Berardi (Bifo) was certainly pointing to was precisely the hope in the chance encounter of revolutionary politics with desire and creation. In that sense, perhaps the names "Negri" and "Guattari" could be said to be bearers of the categories, on the one hand, of revolutionary will and, on the other, of creation and desire.

So this approchement serves merely to mark, with perhaps too far-fetched an image, the way that this book could be read today: as a call to respond to defeat by reaffirming faith in collective revolutionary action; with new forms of organising, new ways of association, and new singularisations of collective subjectivity combining militancy with creativity.

This response to a defeat of a collective movement asks us to recommence thinking a way out from the defeat; recognising the depth of the defeat while at the same time declaring faith in the ideas and practices that characterised the movement. This book can, in many ways, be said to sum up a whole period of theoretical reflection of both theorists – in Guattari's case, his *Molecular Revolution*, *L'Incoscient Machinique*, and *Il capitale mondiale integrato*;[2] and, in Negri's, *Marx Beyond Marx*, *Il comunismo e la guerra*, and *The*

Constitution of Time.[3] To that extent, there are perhaps no theoretical advances in this book – although what an extraordinary confluence of ideas and common interests and desires are to be found here, in this book that emerges, as Negri tells us in his 1990 Postscript, from correspondence between the two authors while the one was in prison.

And yet, what perhaps does become explicit for the first time, is the question of defining and asserting fidelity to the communist project and, most crucially, the start of thinking anew the question of organisation, in a way that will refuse to see these aspects divided into a means/ends dyad. Indeed, it is perhaps this refusal that most clearly marks the text, signalling a course of study and practice that – though cut short in the case of Guattari – will result in *Chaosmose*, The *Three Ecologies* and continues for Negri in his collaborations with Michael Hardt.[4] Themes that were struggling for expression began to be first rehearsed here.

I shall focus this short introduction on the persistence of the question of organisation, but will begin with a few words on the definition of communism.

The book begins with what Negri tells us in his Postscript was something many – including friends, we can only imagine the position of his enemies! – found incomprehensible: 'The project: to rescue "communism" from its own disrepute'. Let me begin with a restatement of the several, cumulative definitions of communism that the authors provide us with in this book. Communism is:

– 'the collective struggle for the liberation of work'
– 'the assortment of social practices leading to the transformation of consciousness and reality on every level: political and social, historical and everyday, conscious and unconscious'
– 'the establishment of a communal life style in which individuality is recognized and truly liberated, not merely opposed to the collective'
– 'the singular expression for the combined

productivity of individuals and groups ("collectivites") emphatically not reducible to each other… the process of singularization'

The gap between *telos* and movement is refused in their account of communism. Militant organisations refuse to see themselves as ones directed to realising an external ideal. They are instead forms that, in the process of their organisation-singularisation, realise communism as integral to that movement. But it is how organisation-communism can be interwoven that is the daunting task to which this small book provides a first response.

What then are these new ways of thinking the question of (communist)organisation that are beginning to emerge? It is, I think, important to consider the statements made by the two authors on this question in the two newly translated essays, one signed "Guattari" the other "Negri" that were published at the end of the original French edition of the book in 1985.[5] Guattari's account is possibly the most fully developed of the two, although Negri provides an interesting difference of viewpoint whose importance is crucial in signalling the contrasting theoretical and practical traditions of thinking and struggle which none the less came together in this remarkable little book.

In the concluding pages of his intervention, Guattari sets out three 'conditions' to which the 'militant assemblages to-come'. First, the

> New social practices of liberation will not establish hierarchical relations between themselves; their development will answer to a principle of transversality that will enable them to be established by traversing, as a rhizome, heterogeneous social groups and interests (p. 123)

That is, these militant assemblages will refuse 'authoritarian discipline, formal hierarchies, orders of priority decreed from above, obligatory ideological reference points....' And yet, a point to which we shall return, this must not be seen as in conflict with what Guattari tells us is the 'obviously inevitable, necessary and desirable establishment of centres of decision that use the most sophisticated technologies of communication and aim to maximum efficaciousness if necessary.' (p. 124) This is clearly a complex and – still unresolved demand – to work out 'analytical collective procedures that enable the separation of the *work of decision* from the *imaginary investments of power*'. Second, one of the principal tasks of these new social practices will be to develop 'collective and/or individual *processes of singularisation*'. Third, these 'mutating militant machines' (p. 125) must be thought not as assemblages built to last and concerned with their self-preservation but should be 'precarious', always in-becoming. And they should do so by 'promoting a logic of multivalent alliances'. They must leave aside the

> perverse myth of the seizing of state power by a vanguard party, without appeal or reservations. Nobody will seize power in the name of the oppressed! Nobody will confiscate freedoms in the name of freedom. The only acceptable objective now is the seizing of society by society itself. (p. 126).

What then of the state? Here Guattari is somewhat ambiguous. The 'mutating militant machines' are not concerned with taking state power, for it is not an 'no exterior monster that one needs to either flee or subdue' (p. 126). The state 'is everywhere, beginning with ourselves, at the root of our unconscious' and to that extent any militant assemblage must contend with it rather than conquering it.

Negri's response is telling of some of the divergences or at least ambiguities that remained between their respective position on the question of organisation and practice which I think it is useful to highlight. On the one hand, Negri reaffirms one of the fundamental principles of *operaismo*: the 'modernisation' or neoliberal restructuring that was underway was merely the

> ... powerful mystification of what we were, of the knowledge that we had... In order to start living again and organize knowledge we must break this totality (p. 132)

That is, Negri links the process of liberation explicitly with the necessity of destruction: 'A positive social practice can be built on this act of destructive freedom today' (p. 132). Negri recognises that the historically and *ontologically* stratified nature of the state makes any notion of its pure and simple destruction, a nonsense; and yet – flirting with Guattari's terminology – he states that its strata can be opened up and be given a different composition which break with the 'capitalist policies of reterritorialisation' (p. 135). But all this takes place within the context of Negri's discussion of the dialectic of liberation and destruction. Is this not Negri's way of saying that the path of liberation must pass through the destruction of the state – however this destruction might be conceived? How else to understand Negri's claim that the 'the concept of the Left is a concept for war' (p. 132) and any attempt to evade this is to render the left 'insignificant'.

We now come to a central aspect of the question of the organisation for liberation, of the form of militant social practice of liberation. This entire discussion revolves around the name, Lenin.

It is clear – more or less explicitly – that when Guattari warns against 'authoritarian disciplines, formal hierarchies, orders of priorities decreed from above, and compulsory ideological references...' (p. 124) he is warning against what we might call the Leninist temptation. At the same time, Guattari recognises, as we have seen, the need for 'centres of decision' within any militant strategy. Largely, this is the question that can be said to define Lenin's thought. It is, arguably, the central contribution made by Lenin to the thought of how militant practice should be organised. The question is clearly, how to think centres of decision outside the form given it in *What is to be Done?* Guattari states merely that such centres of decision will require the utilisation of 'the most sophisticated technologies of communication' for 'maximal effectiveness'. It is not at all clear how this helps us. Guattari and Negri are clear about one thing: they are against 'spontaneist myths', as they write together in *New Lines of Alliance, New Spaces of Liberty*; and even in his contribution to *Pratique de L'Institutionnel et Politique*, he defends *Anti-Oedipus* against attempts to read it as an 'ode to spontaneity or an eulogy to some unruly liberation'.[6] Thus, the debate is put very much in the same terms as the conflict between Lenin's and Luxemburg's problematics of organisation. While all this is true, the means of resolving this question by Guattari and Negri cannot be simply reduced to one side or the other of the debates within the Second International. For Guattari, the refusal of spontaneism was made 'in order to underline the artificial, "constructivist" nature of desire that we [Guattari and Deleuze] defined as "machinic" ... To say of desire that it makes up part of the infrastructure amounts to saying that subjectivity produces reality' (p. 128, 129). But while for Guattari this amounts – implicitly – to a dismissal of Lenin, Negri is much more unwilling to allow such a rapid move beyond Lenin.

In Negri's response to Guattari, he writes:

> ...the history of the party, i.e. the history of the continuous dialectic of class consciousness between institutional "structure" and revolutionary "agency" – the history of the party, from anarchism to social democracy, from socialism to Leninism, finds itself explained by the linear evolution of class composition. Let it be clear that a process of accumulation is actually revealed through this evolution, a subjective movement of categorization, selection, and constitution. What was retained from past consciousness and experiences of organisation served as a critical

material means to formulate an ever renewed project of liberation. (p. 136)

And if his position on Leninism still remains somewhat ambiguous, he states that:

From this new perspective on struggle and organizing, Leninism is no doubt an element to be subsumed, even if it will always be kept alive in the agency that we are preparing (p. 137)

And what is this always living moment of Leninism, this 'stark reminder of the unforgettable function of class war (which cannot be erased or neglected), as an indication of the necessity to destroy the totality of the *dispositif* of command of the enemy – a never-ending task for those in search of liberation' (p. 138). Desire as construction, as machinic, is understood by Negri as the passage from 'movement to party' (p. 140); it depends upon the material force of the masses establishing a relationship between knowledge and the 'capacity for destruction'. The problem, as Negri states it in the final words of his response, is that of 'how to be the catastrophe by building it (p. 141) with Spinoza's affirmation of a love that lies between 'knowledge and power' and 'above all', with the eternal and Goethean Lenin: "in the beginning is action". Let us make haste' (p. 142).

We should, of course, mention Negri's brief comments on this debate in his 1990 Postscript to the English edition of the book reprinted here.[7] Here, the terms of the debate – spontaneity and direction – are linked to the names Luxemburg and Lenin but while restating the central importance of this debate, this time, instead of, as in François Dosse's words, expressing 'his ineradicable attachment to Leninism' (*Gilles Deleuze et Félix Guattari. Biographie Croisée*, F. Dosse, Éditions La Découverte, p. 357), which Dosse sees as characterising Negri's concluding statements in the '*Lettre Archéologique*', Negri states somewhat more ambiguously, that the future movements 'will have to reconsider these issues'.

But we cannot conclude here. More needs to be said about Negri's Lenin. If we are to grasp Negri's continuing reliance upon Lenin for the 'ever renewed project of liberation' (p. 136), and if we are to situate his Lenin within today's Lenin revival associated with the names of Slavoj Žižek, Alain Badiou (via the figure of Saint Paul), Sylvain Lazarus, and others, a brief comparison with some of these new approaches will be instructive.[8] What would have and will seem to many to be, at best, a misplaced nostalgia, at worst, a confirmation of the totalitarian lurking within every communist that reference to the name Lenin evokes, can best be answered through a consideration of his thought that refuses the simple reduction of the meaning of Lenin to state socialism.

For this purpose it is instructive to very briefly indicate where Negri's Lenin distinguishes himself from that of two of the most exciting thinkers of the moment – namely Žižek and Badiou's – appropriation of Lenin. Let us begin with Badiou. What distinguishes his from Negri's Lenin is not that he accepts what Negri calls the position of 'western political science' on Lenin: i.e. '"To speak of Lenin is to speak of the conquest of power"'.[9] It is true that Badiou is quite clear that the question of politics is always a question of power for Lenin, and to think of it in any other terms is utterly naïve.[10] However, as Negri points, it is not the question of the seizure of power itself that is 'repellent',[11] it is the divorcing of the question of seizing power from the 'abolition of the state'. It is clear, however, that for all the shifts in his thinking on the relation the subject should take to the state, from – as Alberto Toscano puts it – from the 'dialectics of destruction' of his Maoist phase, to the notions of 'distance' and 'subtraction' of his later thought,[12] it has never, for Badiou, been a case of the simple capture of state power that characterises the 'repellent' Lenin of western (bourgeois) political science.

In fact, it is Žižek who perhaps best indicates where Badiou's later thinking on politics and the state falls down, and that incidentally takes the same name as one of Negri's great bugbears – as assiduous Negri readers will recognise – namely, in the 'autonomy of the Political' that it reveals. Žižek writes in 'Repeating Lenin: Lenin's Choice':

> No wonder that the Lenin Badiou and Lazarus prefer is the Lenin of *What Is to Be Done?*, the Lenin who (in his thesis that the socialist-revolutionary consciousness has to be brought from without to the working class) breaks with Marx's alleged 'economism' and asserts the autonomy of the Political, NOT the Lenin of *The State and Revolution*, fascinated by the modern centralized industry, imagining the (depoliticized) ways to reorganize economy and the state apparatus. (*Revolution at the gates: a selection of writings from February to October 1917*, Vladimir Illich Lenin and Slavoj Žižek, Verso, p. 271)

This quote is interesting because it manages to sum up not only the differences between Badiou (and Lazarus) and Žižek and Negri, but also between the first two (or three) and Negri. As for Žižek, so for Negri *The State and Revolution* is a more contemporary and relevant text than *What is to be Done?* And this is, at least in part, because the hypostatisation of the political that many have drawn from it results in understanding (misunderstanding I would argue) the critique of economism as a dismissal of political economy. It would, however, be a mistake to accuse Badiou of such a misunderstanding. His own reasons for inserting a radical hiatus between the state and the economic is due to a series of extremely complex ontological set-theoretical reasons.[13] Caricaturising this complex discussion to limits set by this short introduction, whereas the state, society, economics, etc. are the work – ordering – of being, politics is the realm of the event that is irreducible to being. In this way, Lenin is championed by Badiou as the subject of the event of October 1917, an event without socio-economic conditions, or at least, where those conditions are not the conditions of the event named Bolshevik Revolution.[14]

On this score, both Žižek and Negri are in agreement: one cannot divorce economic from political – indeed, Marx's critique of political economy operates a precise insertion of the political into the economic. However, Žižek's conclusion that from *The State and Revolution* one should draw together the strands of the Lenin-political-strategist and Lenin-technocrat of the new society and new state, is equally repellent to Negri. Žižek frequently states that he stands in contrast to Badiou's championing of the moment, the event of 1917 and war communism, affirming instead the project of the patient, laborious construction of socialism (in one country, one might add). But this stress on the technocratic element of Žižek's Lenin, should not be (con-)fused with the Tronti-Cacciari reading of Lenin that so often is the object of Negri's ire.[15] For despite Žižek's rhetorical strategy of provocation – such as his apparent championing of the Lenin of '*Communism is Soviet power plus electrification of the whole country*',[16] of the constructivist image of the cold, disciplined, mechanised new man, etc. – it is the utopian moment that is opened and the battles for socio-cultural-organisational change that excites him about Lenin, and his demand to repeat, not return to Lenin. To that extent at least, Žižek and Negri are not so far from one another.

And yet, a distance remains, and what links Žižek's Lenin to Badiou's is what most opposes him to Negri. Despite Žižek's recognition of the necessary intersection of the political and the socio-economic – that contra Badiou the two cannot be divorced from one another by the anti-ontology of the (revolutionary) event, that 'true heroism resides not in blindly clinging to the early revolutionary enthusiasm [as Badiou does], but in recognizing "the rose in the cross of the present"' of the material conditions one is caught within[17] – nevertheless, Žižek reveals his very own autonomization of the Political:

> With Lenin, as with Lacan, the revolution *ne s'autorise que d'elle meme*: one should assume responsibility for

the revolutionary act not covered by the big Other – the fear of taking power 'prematurely', the search for the guarantee, is the fear of the abyss of the act.[18]

So, while Žižek is arguing – quite correctly – that Lenin refuses the revisionist tendency to await for the 'objective conditions' to develop to a sufficient degree, that the 'stages' of social development unfold, that it is only with the say-so of these conditions, stages, laws that the process of revolution is justified; nevertheless, his challenge to opportunism (to use of good Leninist epithet) that revolution cannot rest upon the big Other, does not amount – as Žižek suggests – to the statement that the revolution must rest on nothing other than itself, the 'abyss of the act', to legitimate itself. Is this not effectively to substitute an ethics of the revolutionary event for a politics? By this move Žižek takes one step forward and two steps back.

Let us return in conclusion to Negri then, and his very own assertion that one should not return to but one should repeat Lenin. To repeat Lenin, then, is yes to affirm what might be termed the subjective moment of political struggle and analysis. But such a 'moment' cannot be condensed in the notion of the act, the moment of decision. As always, for Negri it is a question of class composition.[19] Negri writes:

> ...it is only within this subject that the real relations of forces can be assessed. The entire history of capital is, from this standpoint, the history of class struggles and struggles of the different political class compositions, and it is possible to read in the fabric of struggle the history of capital as its effect.[20]

No materialist conception of the subject can be given other than through the filter of class composition: it is only class composition that gives us the material and political complexity of the figure of the subject.[21]

The notion of class composition draws together two aspects: a technical aspect, which involves an analysis of the world of production, its transformation, and the effects upon the labouring subject including the development of a certain level of needs and desires. The second aspect, the political composition, concerns the ways that this first – at least partly technologically driven – aspect can be appropriated politically. We can – simplifying again – speak of the way the specifics of the objective dynamics of exploitation are appropriated subjectively, i.e. from the standpoint of the working class. Lenin's great contribution was, for Negri, to 'translate the real class composition, as determined specifically, in organisational terms'.[22] But such a contribution rests on more than a political sensibility or 'art of intervening', as Žižek would have it.[23] It means truly following through on, and precisely articulating what it means to recognise that 'the economy is in itself political'.[24] Thus, whereas for Negri as well as for Žižek, *The State and Revolution* is a core text, equally Negri places much greater emphasis on Lenin's analysis of capitalist development and of imperialism in its relation to the composition of the class.[25] For it is precisely in the notion of class composition that economic and political questions can be seen to be most clearly intertwined.

So Negri affirms the following theses that he draws from Marx and Lenin:

> a) the history of capitalism is the history of class struggle and of the figures of class composition;
> b) economics and politics cannot be divorced and class composition is the plane on which they come together most directly;
> c) the subject can only be understood, in properly materialist fashion, via the notion of class composition;
> d) Lenin (building on Marx – 'in a lively, original and yet absolutely faithful way'[26]) 'effected a recognition

of the real and [...] proposed a full circulation between (subversive) political strategy and [...] organisation of the masses'.[27]

A little more should be said about this last, crucial moment d). It affirms that the party is the tool for the production of the antagonistic class subject, necessary for this movement because of the non-reducibility of political to technical class composition. It is precisely the non-linear line of determination from technical to political class composition that Negri draws from Lenin[28] and which allows for a properly revolutionary politics: class composition is freed through the destruction of the class antagonist, and thereby becomes a moment of creation. So not simply the dialectical passage from class composition via its determinate negation vertically raised to the form of revolutionary organisation – but onwards further, the form of revolutionary organisation, through the insurrectionary moment establishing the dictatorship of the proletariat that sets in train a continuous revolutionary movement towards communism. As Negri wrote over 35 years ago, that which:

> ...the organisation *mediates* can be made *immediate* in the behaviour of the working class from the moment that overturning of the class adversary's power, from the moment that the working class and the proletariat as such fully assume the task and weight of the construction of a new revolutionary society.[29]

If this is a correct summary of Negri's Lenin, then it can be argued that Negri remains true to the "Lenin moment" throughout his career. For Negri's texts rest upon a particular analysis of class composition, of the antagonistic subject from which he then operates a translation, or more properly a *creation* of a political form adequate to the demands of the class subject through which the communist impulse is given concrete form. This is most evident in his writings from the 1960s and '70s. But it is equally true of his more recent forays into political economy – into what he calls immaterial labour, cognitive capitalism and biopolitical production, which that mark a particular level of development of the subject that forms an already articulated biopolitical reality, the 'subversive body of this "general intellect"'.[30]

It is not possible to properly evaluate this work in the space remaining but, to conclude, I want to highlight one of the risks of the new analysis – a risk that contains, I believe many of the ambiguities of Negri's later relations to Lenin today. It is the risk of a refounded spontaneism. The question Negri poses is whether, today, socially cooperative immaterial labour can, thanks to its composite nature as communism prefigured, if it can be the 'demiurge of its own body', or whether it requires an external vanguard to 'transform this flesh into a body, the body of the general intellect'.[31] Negri's sympathy for the former option is not in doubt, although he admits that it is a question that can only be decided through a 'genuine movement of struggle'[32] through which it must confirm its superior strength. It is this sympathy that made writing with Guattari all those years ago a possibility. But, if this miraculating of an organisational form is allowed, we may ask once again whether organisation would be anything other than what Negri had condemned as the strategy of revisionist 'process-organisation' in his 1970s book on Lenin? Of course, Negri would point to the transformations in the class composition – the emergence of immaterial labour, of the multitude – to signal the radical difference between conditions today and then (whether referring to early 1900s or to the 1970s); but doubts surely remain that changes in class composition have overcome the need for the instance of emersion from the ocean of productive multiplicities; that the exigency for a vertical – but not transcendent – political moment that slices through the cooperative productivity of the multitude, reconfiguring it in a form able to strike at capital and the practices of governance has been lain to rest. Negri's *33 Lezzioni* includes a beautiful little cautionary passage on this problem, that it is necessary to restate: either 'organisation is spontaneity that reflects upon itself. Otherwise it is impotence and defeat that try to justify themselves'.[33]

New Lines of Alliance, New Spaces of Liberty is a formidable little précis of the political – and theoretical – contradictions and tensions that traverse communist politics. It is these tensions and the relentless struggle for their resolution that continue to make of communist thought the untranscendable horizon for any revolutionary politics of our times.

Notes

1. Many thanks to Stefano Harney and Alberto Toscano for typically perceptive comments to the various drafts of this introduction.
2. *Molecular Revolution: Psychiatry and Politics*, translated by R. Sheed, Penguin, London 1984; *L'incoscient Machinique: Essais de Schizo-analyse*, Recherches, 1979; *Il capitale mondiale integrato*, Cappelli, 1982.
3. Published as the first part in *Time for Revolution*, A. Negri, translated by M. Mandarini, Continuum, London 2003.
4. *Chasmose*, F. Guattari, Galilé, Paris 1982, translated in English as *Chaosmosis*, translated by P. Bains and J. Pefanis, Indiana University Press, Bloomington 1995; *Les Trois Écologie*, F. Guattari, Galilé, Paris 1989, translated in English as *The Three Ecologies*, translated by I. Pindar and P. Sutton, Athlone Press, London 2000. For Negri's co-authored projects, I have in mind particularly *Empire*, Harvard University Press, Cambridge 2000 and *Multitude*, Penguin, New York 2004.
5. The essays, in fact presentations that were composed in view of a conference in Montreal shortly before the book was published, were published in neither the 1989 Italian edition nor the 1990 English edition. They were originally published as addenda to the actual text, entitled *Les Nouveaux Espaces de Liberté*. They are translated here for the first time in English so that we can finally present the complete first edition of the book.
6. Pratique de *L'Institutionnel et Politique*, F. Guattari, J. Oury, F.Tosquelles, Editiones Matrices, 1985, p 62, translated in *The Guattari Reader*, ed. G. Genosko, Blackwell, 1996, p. 128.
7. It should be recalled that both the English and the Italian edition of the text, both published at around the same time, nei-

ther of these concluding essays were included.
8. For an outstanding collection of the variety of new approaches to Lenin, see *Lenin Reloaded: Toward a Politics of Truth*, S. Budgen, S. Kouvelakis, S. Žižek editors, Duke University Press, Durham and London, 2007.
9. 'What to do Today with What is to be Done?, or Rather: The Body of the General Intellect', A. Negri, translated by G. Thomson, in *Lenin Reloaded*, p. 297. The same piece has been published in a different translation in *Reflections on Empire*, A. Negri, translated by E. Emery, Polity, Cambridge 2008. Although Emery's translation of this expression as 'bourgeois political science' (Reflections, p. 148) is incorrect, it could be argued that this is effectively Negri's accusation.
10. 'One Divides Itself into Two, A. Badiou, in *Lenin Reloaded*, p. 12.
11. *Reflections*, p.
12. 'From the State to the World?: Badiou and Anti-capitalism', A. Toscano, *Communication and Cognition*, 37, 3-4, 2004, p. 199.
13. For anyone who wants to acquaint themselves with Badiou's argument, they should turn to *Being and Event*, A. Badiou, translated by O. Feltham, Continuum, London 2005, in particular to Meditation 8 and 9. See also *Metapolitics*, A. Badiou, translated by J. Barker, Verso, London 2005, chapter 5 'Politics Unbound' in particular.
14. Or more precisely still, the event cannot be extracted from those conditions.
15. For some discussion of the debate between Negri and Cacciari and Tronti, see my 'Beyond Nihilism: Notes Towards a Critique of Left-Heideggerianism in Italian Communist Thought,' in *Cosmos & History*, 5:1, 2009.
16. *Collected Works volume 31*, V. I. Lenin, Lawrence & Wishart, London 1966, p. 516.
17. 'Trotsky's *Terrorism and Communism*, or, Despair and Utopia in the Turbulent Year of 1920', S. Žižek, forward to *Terrorism and Communism*, by l. Trotsky, Verso, London 2007, p. xxi.
18. 'Trotsky's *Terrorism and Communism*, or, Despair and Utopia in the Turbulent Year of 1920', p. xviii.
19. For a detailed discussion of the notion of 'class composition', see *Storming Heaven: Class Composition and Struggle in Italian Autonomist Marxism*, S. Wright, Pluto Press, London 2002, and my 'Antagonism vs. Contradiction: Conflict and the Dynamics of Organisation in the Thought of Antonio Negri'

in *Contemporary Organization Theory*, ed. C. Jones and R. Munro, Blackwell, Oxford 2005, and in *The Sociological Review*, Oct. 2005, vol. 53, s.1.
20. *Trentatre Lezioni su Lenin* [1977], A. Negri, Manifestolibri, Roma 2004, p. 23 – my translation.
21. *Dall'Operaio Massa all'Operaio Sociale*, A. Negri, edited by P. Pozzi and R. Tommasini, Multhipla Edizioni, Milan 1979, p. 60 – my translation.
22. 33 Lezioni, p. 23.
23. 'A Leninist Gesture Today', S. Žižek, in *Lenin Reloaded*, p. 83.
24. 'A Leninist Gesture Today', S. Žižek, in *Lenin Reloaded*, p. 91.
25. These aspects are central to Negri's analysis in his book length study of Lenin, *33 Lezioni su Lenin*, initially presented first as lectures over 35 years ago, and return in Negri's discussion of Lenin more recently, such as in his 2001 piece, 'What to do Today with What is to be Done?' in *Lenin Reloaded*.
26. *33 Lezioni*, A. Negri, p. 164 – my translation.
27. 'What to do Today with What is to be Done?', A. Negri, p. 301.
28. To await the economic conditions, to assume that specific economic conditions will immediately determine a political form, this is what Lenin condemned as 'economism', 'spontaneism' and opportunism – submission to the big Other, in Žižek's (via Lacan) take on this eminently political problem.
29. *33 Lezioni*, A. Negri, p. 165.
30. 'What to do Today with What is to be Done?', A. Negri, in *Lenin Reloaded*, p. 301. Negri has explored the new composition of labour in seminars in Paris with Carlo Vercellone, as well as in *Reflections on Empire*, his work with Michael Hardt, and elsewhere. This work is also being pursued by Christian Marazzi, Andrea Fumagalli, Paolo Virno, Maurizio Lazzarato, and many others. The journal *Historical Materialism* has a very useful stream of articles on these themes.
31. 'What to do Today with What is to be Done?', A. Negri, in *Lenin Reloaded*, p. 302.
32. 'What to do Today with What is to be Done?', A. Negri, in *Lenin Reloaded*, p. 302.
33. *33 Lezioni*, A. Negri, p. 42.

1. Communists Like Us

The project: to rescue "communism" from its own disrepute. Once invoked as the liberation of work through mankind's collective creation, communism has instead stifled humanity. We who see in communism the liberation of both collective and individual possibilities must reverse that regimentation of thought and desire which terminates the individual.

Bankrupt: the collectivist regimes have failed to realize socialist or communist ideals. Capitalism too has played fast and loose with promises of liberty, equality, progress and enlightenment. Forget capitalism and socialism: instead we have in place one vast machine, extending over the planet an enslavement of all mankind. Every aspect of human life – work, childhood, love, life, thought, fantasy, art – is deprived of dignity in this workhouse. Everyone feels only the threat of social demise: unemployment, poverty, welfare.

Work itself defaults on its promise of developing the relations between humanity and the material environment; now everyone works furiously, to evade eviction, yet only hastening their own expulsion from the mechanical process that work has become.

Indeed work itself – as organized by capitalism or socialism – has become the intersection of irrational social reproduction and amplified social constraints. Fetters – irrational social constraints – are thus at the foundation of all subjective consciousness formed in the work process. And establishing this collective subjectivity of restriction and surveillance is the first imperative of the capitalist work apparatus. Self-surveillance and doubt prevent any intimations of escape, and preempt any questioning of the political, legal or moral legitimacy of the system. No one can withdraw from this capitalist legality of blindness and absurd goals.

Each instance of work, each sequence, is overdetermined by the imperatives of capitalist reproduction; every action helps to solidify the hierarchies of value and authority.

And yet – why is it that the discussion of communism is taboo? This discourse is defamed and banished by the very people it pretends to liberate from their chains. Could it be due to the seductive, "progressivist" rationality of capitalism and its organization of work?

After all, capitalist work arrangements have succeeded in appropriating the discourse of communism – an analysis of labor and its liberatory power – and reduced it to techniques of manipulation: "Arbeit Macht Frei." Even the socialist varieties trumpet recovery and reconstruction as though these were instrumental goals attainable through technical means. The "ethic" of social revolution has become instead a nightmare of liberation betrayed, and the vision of the future is freighted with a terrible inertia…

Not so long ago, the critique of capitalism was directed at its destructive, penetrating market. Today we submit to its traumatization of our souls, passively assuming that reinvestment strategies are the least oppressive form of planning – and socialism or capitalism becomes a moot point.

So now everything must be reinvented: the purpose of work as well as the modalities of social life, rights as well as freedoms. We will once again begin to define communism as the collective struggle for the liberation of work, that is, at once, an end to the current situation!

Empty-headed economists dominate all over the globe – and yet the planet is devastated, perhaps inexorably. We must affirm first of all that there is more than one path: the path of capitalist imperium and/or socialist/collectivist work forms whose persistence and vitality depend to a large part on our own incapacity to redefine work as a project and a process of liberation. We will define communism as the assortment of social practices leading to the transformation of consciousness and reality on every level: political and social, historical and everyday, conscious and unconscious. Recognizing that discourse is action, we will forge a new discourse in such a fashion as to initiate the destruction of the old way. But our communism will not for all that be a spectre haunting the old Europe... We rather envisage an imaginative, creative process at once singular and collective, sweeping the world with a great wave of refusal and of hope. Communism is nothing other than a call to life: to break the encirclement of the capitalist and socialist organization of work, which today leads not only to a continuing surplus of repression and exploitation, but to the extinction of the world and humanity with it.

Exploitation has advanced, on the basis of nuclear accumulation, to become a threat of execution; the cycles of war and the danger of destruction are well known. Now we are not determinists – but today it is not only determinists who recognize that the end is, if not near, certainly close by, especially if we abandon power to the capitalist and socialist juggernauts of labor. Preventing catastrophe will require a collective mobilization for freedom. Why does everyday life tremble with fear and loathing? This fear is not the state of nature as described by Hobbes – that old excuse of the war of all against all, individual wills fragmented in a thirst for power. Rather what we have now is a transcendental, yet actually man made fear which seeps into every mind with immobilizing, catastrophic dread. Indeed hope itself has fled this hopeless, hapless, grey world. Beyond malaise, life sinks into sadness, boredom and monotony, with no chance to break out of the morass of absurdity. Communication – speech, conversation, banter, even conspiracy has all been taken in by the discourse of mass media. Interpersonal relations likewise have spoiled, and are now characterized by indifference, disingenuous disgust and self-hatred – in a word, we're all suffering from bad faith.

Amazingly, the fabric of human feelings has itself come unraveled, since it no longer succeeds in connecting the threads of desire and hope. As a result, this pseudo-war has passed over the world for thirty years without its key features being noticed; the Cold War escapes unrecognized as the true culprit.

During that whole time, human consciousness has been ground down into something more manageable, even complicit. As the individual sinks into isolated despair, all the built up values in the world collapse around him. Fear breeds impotence and paralysis of every sort. Only this collective stupefaction prevents onrushing despair from reaching its logical conclusion in collective suicide; apparently there's not enough passion left for such a crisp transformation. But the real tragedy is that exploitation masquerades as fear: individual extensions – of desires and hopes for the future – have been simply prohibited, but under a metaphysical, rather than political guise.

And yet. And yet all the developments in the sciences and in the productive capacities of labor point to the existence of an alternative. Extermination or communism is the choice – but this communism must be more than just the sharing of wealth (who wants all this shit?) – it must inaugurate a whole new way of working together.

Real communism consists in creating the conditions for human renewal: activities in which people can develop themselves as they produce, organizations in which the individual is valuable rather than functional. Accomplishing this requires a movement – to change the character of work itself. And redefining work as creative activity can only happen as individuals emerge from stifled, emotionally blocked rhythms of constraint. It will take more than the will to change, in the current situation; to resist neutralization itself demands desire.

Paradoxical as it seems, work can be liberated because it is essentially the one human mode of existence which is simultaneously collective, rational and interdependent. It generates solidarity. Capitalism and socialism have only succeeded in subjugating work to a social mechanism which is logocentric or paranoid, authoritarian and potentially destructive. By means of progressive struggles, workers in the advanced industrial countries have succeeded in lowering the threshold of direct and dangerous exploitation; but this has been countered by changes in the character of that domination. Modern exploitation accentuates the disparity between rich and poor countries – now it is unfree workers in underdeveloped nations who bear the brunt of exploitation through violence and the threat of hunger. The relative improvement in the situation of the metropolitan proletariat is balanced by extermination in the Third and Fourth Worlds. As contradictions built into work have proceeded to their limit, it is not an accident that the liberation of work can now be accomplished by workers in the most advanced sectors of science and technology. What is at stake is the fundamental ability of communities, racial and social groups, indeed minorities of every kind to conquer and establish autonomous modes of expression – not just lifestyles, but the work process itself.

There is nothing inevitable about work – no destiny leads work into ever greater repressions. In fact, the potential for liberation inherent in work itself is more visible than ever. How can capital continue to present its work process as natural and unchangeable, when for technical reasons it is changing every day? This unexamined gap in the logic of work is the opening through which new movements of social transformation will charge pell mell.

Traditionally, the refusal to work, as an instance of struggle and as spontaneous action, has aimed at those structures which are obstacles to the real liberation of work. From now on, that struggle involves appropriating a new capital, that of a collective intelligence gained in freedom, the experience and knowledge that comes from breaking down the one dimensional experience of present day capitalism. This involves all projects of awakening and building towards liberation; in short, anything that helps reclaim mastery over work time, the essential component of life time. All the current catchwords of capitalist production invoke this same strategy: the revolutionary diffusion of information technologies among a new collective subjectivity. This is the new terrain of struggle, and it is not utopian to believe that consciousness itself is the "swing voter" deciding if capitalist or non-capitalist roads are taken. Once, knowledge and power were stockpiled like so many canon or missiles; now the empowering of a collective consciousness, part of the turmoil of the workplace, threatens to unite small arms into a mass revolt.

From this perspective, communism is the establishment of a communal life style in which individuality is recognized and truly liberated, not merely opposed to the collective. That's the most important lesson: that the construction of healthy communities begins and ends with unique personalities, that the collective potential is realized only when the singular is free. This insight is fundamental to the liberation of work. Work as exploitation has completed its development of the general, the mass, the production line; what's now possible is to tap into the potential of individual creative energies, previously suppressed. Nothing less than a genetic breakthrough, this rhizome of autonomy in the workplace can establish itself as a productive enhancement – and a serious challenge to the dead weight of bureaucratic capitalism with its overcoded and de-individualized individual.

Make no mistake about it: communism is not a blind, reductionist collectivism dependent on repression. It is the singular expression for the combined productivity of individuals and groups (collectivities) emphatically not reducible to each other. If it is not a continuous reaffirmation of singularity, then it is nothing – and so it is not paradoxical to define communism as the process of singularization. Communism cannot be reduced in any way whatsoever to an ideological belief system, a simple legal contract, or even to an abstract egalitarianism. It is part of a continuous process which runs throughout history, entailing a questioning of the collective goals of work itself.

Glimpses of these new alliances are already available. They began to form and seek each other out at the time of the spontaneist and creative phase, which of course developed parallel to the big break-up and realignment in capitalist society to which we have been witness over the past three decades. To better locate and appreciate their importance, one can distinguish:

* molar antagonisms: struggles in the workplace over exploitation, criticisms of the organization of work, of its form, from the perspective of liberation;

* molecular proliferations of these isolated instances of struggle into the outside world, in which singular struggles irreversibly transform the relations between individuals and collectivities on the one hand, material nature and linguistic signs (meanings) on the other.

Thus the maturing social transformations, which in turn affect productive work arrangements, are induced, piecemeal, by each and every molar antagonism: any struggle against capitalist and/or socialist power formations contributes to overall transformation. Social, political and workplace advances condition each other. But, and this is our point, the revolutionary transformation occurs in the creation of a new subjective consciousness born of the collective work experience – this moment is primary, all stakes are won or lost here, in the collective creation of subjectivity by individuals. We need to save the glorious dream of communism from Jacobin mystifications and Stalinist nightmares alike; let's give it back this power of articulation: an alliance, between the liberation of work and the liberation of subjectivity.

Singularity, autonomy, and freedom are the three banners which unite in solidarity every struggle against the capitalist and/ or socialist orders. From now on, this alliance invents new forms of freedom, in the emancipation of work and in the work of emancipation.

2. THE REVOLUTION BEGAN IN 1968

I. SOCIALIZED PRODUCTION

It is not necessary to sit reading in a café to realize that the cycle of revolution reopened in 1968, and indeed achieved its high water mark of intensity. What was only an indication in 1917, and which subsequent wars of national liberation failed to achieve in any lasting way, was brought to light by the events of 1968 as the immediate possibility of collective consciousness and action. Yes, communism is possible. It is true, more now than ever, that it haunts the old world. 1968 revealed the fragility of the social contracts installed successively to contain the revolutionary movements of the beginning of the century, those which followed the big crisis of 1929 and the movements which accompanied and followed the second great imperialist war. However one views the events of 1968, it is undeniable that they revealed the failure of this social compromise to eliminate or supersede the antagonistic contradictions of the capitalist systems.

We will now examine the three series of material transformations which concern the quality, the dimensions, and the form of capitalist "producing," and by doing so, highlight those new objective starting points from which any effort to change society will have to begin.

The quality of producing. The struggle between the working classes and those of the capitalist and/or socialist bosses had resulted in a system of production that was more concentrated and massified. The impossibility of rationally overcoming crises, which revealed the social polarization of power, led to the efforts at managing the strongly centralized, planned economies, both capitalist and socialist. In this new environment, the classical law of value no longer operated as an expression of the relation between concrete real labor and amounts of money needed to secure an existence. The new version of the law instead related huge masses of abstract or undifferentiated labor to the ethereal information machines which supplant industrial production. Labor is deterritorialized – without foundation or meaning, it neurotically succumbs to a process which deprives working people of knowledge even as it is essentially knowledge creating activity in the first place. Modern work was creating a global, infernal disciplinary apparatus, in which the constraints were invisible: educational and information constraints which placed the worker at all times under the sway of capital. No longer an eight hour wage slave, the worker now produced and consumed continuously for capital. Capital in the process became more socialized, advancing social cooperation, integrating the collective forces of labor even as it turned society into a giant factory, in which the pacified consuming classes were organized into unions.

Deterritorialized production signifies that work and life are no longer separate; society is collapsed into the logic and processes of capitalist development. The consequences of this assimilation of society to work are profound: All the guarantees and resources of the welfare state – (wage systems, unemployment insurance, family assistance, pensions etc. – were intensified, but now they became part of the production process itself, rather than social defenses against capitalist dislocations. Social welfare in fact became a social dream: as the production process remade society in its own image, that high degree of abstraction was transferred to social life. Production now conferred membership in society. As the independent variable, production stamps society with its characteristic, leaving no region untouched. An equation is established, in which capitalist advancement and exploitation are seen as essential features of social machinery – that this is the meaning of society, and of course it has become true...

The political consequences of this transformation are equally profound. A high degree of political mobilization, evident in the demand for political participation growing out of a century of revolution and class consciousness, has expanded but then dissipated into a social consciousness. All the efforts of the bosses, who are conscious of this new socialization, consist of maintaining it – either through democratic or totalitarian means – within the framework of institutions and of rules for dividing the social product, which permit them to reproduce and thus to reinforce their commanding positions, in a manner that transforms economic into political power.

Before examining the consequences of this transformation of command, it is important to recognize another essential aspect of the changing character of production. The emergence of socialization as a crucial component of production has naturally affected the production process itself. Socialization, typically viewed as a formal quality, mutates into a substantive one: One may observe, for example, how the socialization of rural peasants accompanies their loss of independence, or how service sector workers lose social cohesion as they are functionally absorbed into rigid, mechanized production processes. Up to this point, however, the industrial modes of production associated with capitalism and socialism had only taken possession of social inequalities from the outside, so to speak. The great conflagration of 1968 demonstrated that the new economic techniques now implicated the domain of social reproduction. Before then, the world of production was based on exchange values (commodity production) and the reproduction of use value (utility). All that is over. In this regard, one could consider the movements of that period as necessary preliminaries...

Now the remaining private sphere – family, personal life, free time, and perhaps even fantasy and dreams –

everything from that point on became subjected to the semiotics of capital. This transformation took place regardless of political climate: democratic, fascist, socialist. Socialized production succeeded in imposing its law, its logic, on every facet of social life on earth, vampiristically appropriating free time, the lifeblood of humanity.

The events of 1968 posed themselves as an antagonistic recognition of this transformation of the social quality of production and work procedures. In a chaotic but nonetheless convincing way, they revealed the fundamental contradiction at the base of these transformations, that of conferring an immense productive capability to humanity while at the same time imposing a new proletarian destiny. This destiny originated in permanent expropriation, in the deterritorialization that allows no home base, no solidarity, no recourse, no guarantees, and extends not only throughout social life but into the unconscious.

Generalized exploitation, at all levels of society, had the effect of redefining production as the source of new, supplemental sources of unhappiness, and correspondingly new forms of political, even micro-political conflict. The new modes of production – integrative, totalizing, subtly totalitarian – effectively transformed the old modes of economic slavery into thinly disguised cultural and political subjection. A struggle ensued, which attempted to reduce all resistance against the supposed economic necessity to powerlessness. But it is precisely this transfer of "totalitarist" objectives to the minute, molecular levels of everyday existence which gives rise in turn to new forms of resistance on these most immediate levels, throwing into relief the entire problem of individual and collective isolation.

In 1968, this new "reactivity" expressed itself in the form of a tremendous short circuit. It would be useless to try to mystify these events, as the softheads of recovery have tried. It would be useless at this point to stigmatize the return of the great monsoons of irrationality. And what would such references to rationality signify anyway, in a world in which functionalism is strictly geared toward capital, which in itself constitutes a maximization of irrationality? The question which remains posed since 1968 is rather that of knowing how to establish a creative and liberating relation between happiness and instrumental reason.

From 1968 on, we have also witnessed an inversion of the cycle of struggles against colonialism and underdevelopment, and some attempts at internal modernization have appeared, on the part of the more dynamic sectors of the capitalist and socialist bourgeoisies. But there is a big difference between these ideological efforts – lip service, basically – and the realities of exploitation and new forms of concrete resistance.

1968 expresses the actual reopening of a critical consciousness, itself the crystallization of objective changes within the workforce and production generally. This recognition appeared at first as rebellion, and as a new opening itself made possible by economic growth, its impasse, crisis, and the consequent reflexes of rejection. The essential force of 1968 resides in the fact that for the first time in the history of human revolts against exploitation, the objective was not simple emancipation, but a true liberation, extending beyond the removal of obvious, individual chains. The movements attained a global level reflected in a heightened consciousness of the historical linkage of singular struggles. For the first time at that level of intensity, the molar macrocosms and the molecular microcosms – the global and the local – began to combine in the same subversive whirlwind.

The events of 1968 thus mark the reopening of a revolutionary cycle. Not by the repetition of old slogans, but through the intervention of new perspectives on action, and by a redefinition of communism as enrichment, diversification of community and consciousness. Certainly the movement remained inseparable from the development of previous social struggles, and the redeployment of the employers' capacity for resistance and attack, but an important historical qualitative leap nevertheless occurred. At that point of individual radical fulfillment, what was required to generalize revolution among a significant portion of the population? Nothing short of a social cyclotron: the generation of an immense collective energy, the acceleration of ideas and emotions. In 1968, a revolution worthy of the most authentic aspirations of humanity was born.

II. BEYOND POLITICS

At the time of these movements, the refusal by living social labor of the organization of profit-based capitalism and/or socialism began to spread into the political arena. From a multiplicity of singular conflicts a grand opposition arose, directly confronting the political power responsible for administering social production. Traditional politics found itself completely cut off from this mass movement of collective consciousness; it shared no ground with the transformation of subjectivity. Traditional politics succeeded in grasping it only from the outside, by attempting to stall, repress, and finally to restructure and recover on its own. But by this very misapprehension and denial, it merely demonstrated its own powerlessness.

Politics today is nothing more than the expression of the domination of dead structures over the entire range of living production. A short time ago, at the end of the great revolutionary periods, history witnessed similar political restorations, which had no other goal than to "cover" the fundamental absence of legitimacy on the part of the elites who regained power. The princes who govern us seem to have returned, in the most absurd of ways, on the same perverse and empty stages, in the same vicious cycles which appeared in the aftermath of the Great Revolution and the Napoleonic epoch. (It is sufficient here to cite *The Charterhouse of Parma*.)

And Hegel's remark comes to mind: "This temple decidedly lacks religion, Germany lacks metaphysics, Europe humanity, reformism imagination..."

On the other hand, the collective imagination remains alive, but it can no longer conceive of politics outside of the paradigms and avenues of change which began to appear in 1968.

This is true first of all for the traditional left. The historical communist parties, prisoners of antiquated paradigms of production, did not even succeed in imagining the revolutionary force of the social mode of production which was in the process of emerging. Incapable of separating themselves from centralist organizational models deriving from a paradigmatic split between the avant-garde and the masses, they found themselves disoriented and frightened in the face of the unexpected self-organization of a social movement.

Loyal to the one-dimensional destiny of the reformist movement, they experienced the explosion of new demands in the workplace, and of new desires in the sociocultural world, as a catastrophe which literally left them in a paranoid state. The same applies to a lesser degree to social democratic forces.

In the "actually existing socialist" countries, the reaction was extremely brutal, while in the West, it was more insidious, maneuverable, willing to compromise. In all of these instances, one finds the same invariants: – social conservatism, combined with a systematic corporatist effort to channel and co-opt struggles; – political reaction, combining a recourse to state power with an appeal to traditional structures, in an attempt to reestablish the legitimacy of the old "elites"; – the squandering of collective subjectivity, in particular through intense use of the mass media, governmental agencies, and the welfare state as a whole.

In fact, the left parties have been devastated by the effects of the movement of 1968 and, even more so, by the collective-singular movements which have emerged since then as the bearers of social transformation. The left has attached itself even more to the traditional statist structures; and in doing so it has jettisoned its own relationship of conflict and compromise, and thus its own basis of legitimacy. But these structures were irrevocably altered by the counter-attacks of 1968; from then on, the old politics could no longer hide its cadaverous face. The constitutional and institutional structures of developed countries east and west find themselves to be doubly undermined: from the inside, by their severe inability to adapt; and from outside, by the new forms of labor protest, reflected in the increase of marginal and part-time precarious workers, as well as other numerous minorities who reject the status quo. This impasse has precluded any possibility of renewal.

All "progressive" capitalist perspectives, which would have involved increased popular participation, were systematically blocked. Constitutional structures, whether they be capitalist or socialist, democratic or totalitarian, have certainly experienced change, but typically in negative terms, always cut off from social movements whose effects they endure, and always by mystifying the actual operation of the system of political representation.

Attempting to respond to this decline in the institutions of popular political representation, power has resorted to techniques of anticipation and substitution, opting for symbolic simulation, adaptation and control. At the moment when the whole of society was finally absorbed into production, and the entirety of working and everyday life was exposed as fundamentally political, that political character was repressed, denied and manipulated. What a gothic sort of society which can maintain as its only ideal a vision of castles and courts completely removed from all real life, these small aristocratic universes which are blind to the new aspirations for freedom, new territorialities striving for autonomy! But how else can one describe these political aristocracies when, from their fortresses, they attempt to impose a stratification of society, devoid of consistency, substituting instead a general arrogance, an indifferent cruelty?

Disease, corruption, plague and madness spread within these closed universes just as they did in the ruling houses of the *ancien regime*. But their time is running out: we are at the threshold between suffering and the moment when history's potential will realize itself. The paralysis of political structures and all the current governmental "difficulties" are both symptoms and specific traits of moribund power formations; they are incapable of adjusting to the movements of society.

There is no doubt that these problems were initiated by the movements of the 1960s. In fact, that was the moment when the surging tide of social struggles arrived at history's center stage. Since that time, as we shall see, the attempts to regain control of the situation have been numerous. But they were all short-lived because the political crisis was not, as the reactionary right assumed, the result of simple economic imbalances, having nothing to do with politics, but rather due to the inability of institutions to transform themselves. The roots of the crisis of politics were social. The current silence of the political forms of opposition reflect a curious neutralization: a canceling out effected by the mutual interference of different components of social production, each of which is itself thoroughly disturbed and undergoing transformation. The so-called "death of politics," of which one hears so much, is only the expression of a new world which is emerging and which employs new and different modes of material and cultural self-valorization – either through entirely external means or peripherally to the dominant power formation, but which, in any event, are antagonistic to it. It is thus a world in the process of change which began its expansion in 1968 and which, since then, through a process of continuous mutation, including all sorts of failures and successes, has struggled to weave a new network of alliances at the heart of the multiplicity of isolated singular components comprising it.

This is the new politics: the need to recharacterize the fundamental struggles in terms of a continuous conquest of (new) arenas of freedom, democracy, and of creativity. And, whatever the militants and the intellectuals who have "given up on all that" may say, there is nothing anachronistic or retrograde or anarchist in this way of conceiving things; indeed, it attempts to understand contemporary social transformations – including their contradictions – on the basis of the productive activities, the desires, and the real needs which regulate them. What is on the other hand entirely irrational and mad is the power of the State, as it has evolved since the 60s, into a sort of lunar Stalinism which only multiplies ad nauseam its rigidity and its institutional paralysis. The ferocious will to a "death of politics" is nowhere more dominant than in the glacial palaces of power.

Although much of it is empty and mystified, this type of power is nonetheless terribly effective. Moreover, one should not underestimate or overlook the great mass of pain and anguish that lies concealed behind its cynicism and its technocratic indifference: the insecurity of everyday life, the precariousness of employment, the fragility of civil rights, and, perhaps most of all, the impossibility of locating meaning in individual and collective life, the de facto banning of communitarian projects, of all "creative becomings" from establishing themselves on their own terms. This pain, which accompanies the lack of humanity in the capitalist brand of subjectivity, can be converted into an infinite array of reaction formations and paradoxical symptoms: inhibitions, evasions of all sorts, but sabotage as well, the transformation of refusal into hatred. This to-and-fro movement reaches its limit when the fear of destruction articulates a consciousness of the madness of power; then the pain itself becomes the vertigo of annihilation. This monstrous will to death in all its different forms today constitutes the true character of politics and the true cause of human misery.

III. THE NEW SUBJECTIVITIES

Since the 1960s, new collective subjectivities have been affirmed in the dramas of social transformation. We have noted what they owe to modifications in the organization of work and to developments in socialization; we have tried to establish that the antagonisms which they contain are no longer recuperable within the traditional horizon of the political. But it remains to be demonstrated that the innovations of the 1960s should above all be understood within the universe of consciousnesses, of desires, and of modes of behavior. It is on this level that the changes became definitively irreversible. These new modes of consciousness have literally dislocated the old scenarios of class struggle by invading the imaginary and cognitive roots of productive activity, transforming the consciousness that corresponds to that activity into an act of transformative individual will. Along the way this individuation of desire has thus spread to the realm of collective practices, which now constitute the new political territories. The dramatic and tumultuous affirmation of desire puts our social living into question and makes it the basis of a higher subjective expression of the ensemble of material and semiotic systems of production. Its opposition to private property is a radical negation of all forms of blind collectivism in capitalist and/or socialist undertakings, and its refusal of work on command actually expresses the will of a higher level of social production.

All seeming connections between this refusal and the massification of social subjectivity must be broken; the relation must be reduced to a paradox, by virtue of which the poverty of this massification is confronted with the most singular processes of subjective will.

Communism has nothing to do with the collectivist barbarism that has come into existence. Communism is the most intense experience of subjectivity, the maximization of the processes of singularization – individuation which represent the capability potential of our collective stock. No universality of man can be extracted from the naked abstraction of social value.

Communism no longer has anything to do with any of this. It is a matter rather of manifesting the singular as multiplicity, mobility, spatio-temporal variability and creativity. That today is the only value on the basis of which one can reconstruct work. A work which no longer is crystallized in the form of private property, which does not consider the instruments of production as ends in themselves, but as means for attaining the happiness of singularity and its expansion in machinic rhizomes – abstract and/or concrete. A work which refuses hierarchical command and which in doing so poses the problem of power, clarifies the functions of deception and exploitation in society, and refuses all compromise, all mediation between its own existence and productivity. (All of which implies redefining the concept of work as the transformations and arrangements of production within the frame of immediate liberation efforts.) New modalities of collective subjectivity themselves bring together these qualities and these desires which change relative to productivity. The new production of subjectivity conceives of power from this point on solely as an horizon of the collective liberation of singularities and as work oriented toward that end – in other words, as self-valorization and self-production of singularities.

The social struggles which exploded in 1968 and in the years following conferred a tremendous power on the coming-to-awareness of students and young people, the women's movement, the environmental and nature first movements, the demand for cultural, racial and sexual pluralism, and also the attempts to renovate the traditional conceptions of social struggle, beginning with that of workers. All too often these experiences have been described in terms of marginality. Marginality was quickly drawn toward the center, and the minoritarian demands succeeded – with difficulty – in detaching themselves from those of the lifeless middle ground. And yet each of them, by following its own course and by articulating its own discourse, potentially represents the needs of the large majority.

Potentially, but in a way that is not any the less efficacious: By taking hold of society as a whole, productive socialization wanted to confer on individuals, communities, and their reciprocal relations the character of universality. But the universality with which they were decked out didn't suit them in the least! Instead of a well-fitting hat, it is a mask, a cowl which only disfigures the expression of their needs, their interests, and their desires. It is not a paradox to say that only the marginalities are capable of universality, or, if you prefer, of movements which create universality. Universal politics are not capable of any transcendent truth; they are not independent of the games of economic valorization; they are inseparable from specific territories of power and of human desire. Political universality cannot therefore be developed through a dialectic of ally/enemy as the reactionary Jacobin tradition competitively prescribes. Truth "with a universal meaning" is constituted by the discovery of the friend in its singularity, of the other in its irreducible heterogeneity, of the interdependent community in the respect for its appropriate values and ends. This is the method and the logic of the marginalities which are thus the exemplary sign of a political innovation corresponding to the revolutionary transformations called forth by the current productive arrangements.

Every marginality, by placing its stakes on itself, is therefore the potential bearer of the needs and desires of the large majority. Before 1968, the problem of reproduction remained marginal in relation to production. The women's movement has made it central. Although the questions relating to the preparation of the abstract and immaterial labor force remained lateral in relation to the factory labor force, the student movements made them central in the same way as the new needs which the theoretical and aesthetic imagination proposed. The emerging collective consciousness came thereby to see itself as the nodal articulation of a multitude of marginalities and singularities; it began to confirm its power on the scale of a significant social-experience, which did not close back on itself or conclude, but which opened out onto further struggles, the proliferation of processes of collective singularization and the infinitely differentiated phylum of their ongoing transformation.

This imagination of liberation thus undertook, with more or less success, to superimpose – and to impose itself – on the fiction of the dominant realities. Its lines of collective feeling, its "new softness," its capacity to bring together the most immediate preoccupations with the broadest social dimensions demonstrated that the emerging forms of production were not the enemy of desire, liberation, and creativity, but only of the capitalist and/or socialist organization of work for profit. Human goals and the values of desire must from this point on orient and characterize production. Not the reverse. During this period, the production of liberation became the foremost goal. It will probably take some time before one can grasp the full significance of what was then at stake. To repeat, it had nothing at all to do with utopianism, but with the intrinsic reality of that historical period's social movement. It was probably the women's movement, with its extraordinary power of development, which, after 1968, most advanced the new synthesis of the concept of production and of social liberation. For the first time, with that degree of lucidity, production for profit and work for the reproduction of the species were overturned, revolutionized on the basis of the most extreme singularity, that of the total conception of the child and of generating a new softness to life.

But this incredible experience was also a symbol: the revolution was understood as an optimization of singularities, as the beginning of a mobilization against the disaster of the current situation and its forms of command. The corporeality of liberation became primary. Insurrection of bodies as an expression of subjectivity, as incarnating the materiality of desires and of needs, as promising in the future the impossibility of separating the collective character of economic development from the singularity of its ends. Insurrection of bodies, meaning the successful liberation of those immense productive forces which humanity, up to this point, only turned against itself. 1968 represents the subjective side of production; this is an interpretation, on a large scale, of its social texture, which displaces the previous political problematics onto the terrain of representation considered as a singular project of liberation.

1968 is also a magnificent reaffirmation of democracy. The fact that it was crossed by a certain naive Rousseauism, that through it a few last champions of Jacobinism and of a disfigured Leninism came to shine forth for a few moments, doesn't in any way detract from the power of democracy in the movement considered in itself. It showed that the proletariat, from this point on, socialized and singularized, would not be able to comprehend a political movement except on the condition that it is founded on democratic arrangements in action. This was not only a theoretical truth but also a concrete historical affirmation: there is no specific form of freedom which is not attached to the group goals of the movement and lived, experienced, by its members. This new given was underscored in a certain way, ontologically, in the generation which came after 1968. And which wants today to send us back to the school of Anglo-American liberalism and its ideas of the marketplace! Anticapitalism and antisocialism have become the only forms which permit a renaissance of democracy.

3. THE REACTION OF THE 1970S: NO FUTURE

I. INTEGRATED WORLD CAPITALISM

A restructuring of power helped to restore the command mechanisms in the 1970s, and to restart the process of capitalist and socialist productive accumulation. Politics and economics, capital and the state, were now completely integrated. The process developed in two directions.

In the first place, as the international integration of national economies on an increasingly world scale, and their subordination within a polycentric and rigorously planned project of control. We call this figure of command which coordinates yet exasperates the unity of the world market, submitting it to instruments of productive planning, monetary control, political influence, with quasi-statist characteristics, Integrated World Capitalism (IWC). In this process, world capital integrates, besides the developed countries and directly dependent on them, the ensemble of real socialist countries, and controls, in addition, the means by which the economies of numerous Third World countries are absorbed, putting in question their previous position of "peripheral dependence." Indeed, statist command and the national states thus undergo a veritable deterritorialization. Integrated World Capitalism is not limited to recomposing, using new forms of unification, the flux and hierarchies of statist powers in their traditional sense. It generates supplementary statist functions which are expressed through a network of international organizations, a planetary strategy of the mass media, rigorous taking control of the market, of technologies, etc.

It is certainly important to avoid an ingenuous or anthropomorphic conception of IWC which would entail describing it as the work of a Leviathan or as a one-dimensional macro-structure of the Marcusean variety. Its planetary expansion, as well as its molecular infiltration, occur through mechanisms which can be extremely flexible and which can even take contractual forms. Each one engages legal forms that rely on continuous procedures rather than constraining substantive law. But it is no less true that it is this very procedural and regulatory continuum of relations which consolidates the centripetal tendency of the system, by diluting and "negotiating" the effect of crises in time and space and by relativistically reterritorializing each singular process.

In the second place, and conditioning the constitution of this global integration, the restructuring aims at the mode of production and the ensemble making up the collective labor force which relates to it. This deterritorialization and this integration was facilitated by rendering the social into data form, i.e. on the basis of the fundamental computerization [*informatisation*] of society. Exploitation could thus be articulated scientifically over the entire arena of the social, extending the control of profit creation mechanisms. Under these conditions, the assembly line of commercial and industrial production spreads its fabric over the social, not in its symbolic sense but materially. Society is no longer merely subsumed by capitalist command; it is absorbed entirely by the integrated mode of production. Differences in productivity and in levels of exploitation can then be articulated in a smoother, more diffuse way within each geopolitical segment according to region, country, or continent. Competition, the key link in the bourgeois market, is no longer very important for this process of capitalist retraining.

The transnational computerization of the social is concerned with only one form of competition: that which it can provoke between workers and between the different strata of the working class and of the proletariat. It thus becomes possible for Integrated World Capitalism to activate specific techniques of analysis and control of social classes – which now make struggles erupt, now pulverize their power at those points where their level of politicization is significant, or, on the contrary, unleash them in a controlled way at those points where the problems of economic take off and of political reform are posed most urgently.

As it has always been in the history of capital, this renovation of the forms of command by Integrated World Capitalism goes hand in hand with a redefinition of the ways surplus value is extracted (computerization of the work process, spread of social control through mass media, subjective integration by governmental apparatuses, etc…).

And as it has always been in the history of the exploitation of workers' struggles, this leap forward of the organization of work and of the state was anticipated by the movements of the class struggle. The forms of social subjectivity which emerged in 1968 gave rise to a weaving of molecular struggles for liberation which are concerned with objectives that are at once immediate and long-term, local, everyday, trivial, yet engaged nevertheless with the future of humanity on a global scale. This operation was of course very complex and, in many respects, impossible to sum up within the framework of a single historical sequence.

It is no less true that the pseudo-progressive dialectic of capitalism which triumphed after the second world war was thus completely blocked. After 1968, the dynamic between the different functions of capital (constant and variable) and the interaction between the class of capitalists and the social work force has radically changed context; this is a result of the emergence of increasingly important, heterogeneous arrangements of subjectivity and sensibility. The law of value has ceased to function – if it ever worked in the manner in which it was described – along with norms of economic proportionality and even the ordinary modalities of simple class exploitation. The social hegemony of the new proletarian subjectivities, once it was affirmed, had to acquire the quality of irreversibility: no longer would anything be able to prevent it from revealing itself, regardless of the prevailing relations of force, "the highs and the lows;" indeed, particularly on the front of their affirmation in the mass media, no longer can anything prevent these subjectivities from being basic reference points for future struggles. Capitalist and/or socialist restructuration does not automatically refer to relatively rational laws. It is not scientific – no matter how sophisticated the theoretical devices and the instruments of prediction which it employs: it is essentially repressive. The computerization [*informatisation*] of the social is inseparable from its mechanization and its militarization, in such a way that the systematic production of information tends to be substituted for the search for it. Such are the zones of strategic importance that the circuits of reproduction which support life and the struggle are more and more controlled, ordered, and, ultimately, repressed in a preventive fashion. Life time thus finds itself tightly fastened onto the military time of capital.

The time of capital, or the capacity to translate every sequence of life into terms of exchange, and of overdetermination with the urgency and the necessity of the operations of economic quantification and of political command; terror, or the capacity to annihilate all those who refuse to submit to it: this is what the reshuffling of the traditional functions of the state, and their unlimited penetration of people's attitudes, sensibility and minds, amounts to. By threatening the very foundations of being, the state manages to control the singular flow of our lives, subjecting it to the rhythm of capitalistic time. Once it became clear that no law, nor other norm, could ever mediate between the capital and the proliferation of collective subjectivities, terror became the only way to secure the resumption to capitalistic and socialistic accumulation in the 1970s. It is under the impetus of this terror that the nuclear state became the central figure of Integrated World Capitalism.

At present the club of nuclear powers subjects on a large scale all nations and peoples to its multicentered networks; but it also dictates in details the countless conflicts and local strifes which poison life on this earth, repressing or fueling them at will. In the Third World, since the so-called period of decolonization, all these conflicts make up some kind of world war that doesn't dare call itself by that name. Nuclear terror is at the root of every kind of oppression and overdetermines the relationships of exploitation between social groups at both political and micropolitical levels. Thus threat and intimidation seep through all the pores of the thin skin of nuclear deterrence, which doesn't exclude more direct forms of intervention. The ultimate goal, as always, is to force people to condone their misery and political impotence. Capitalism answers: "No future" to the rise of new forms of proletarian subjectivity, countering their offensive with state terror. At this juncture the word "democracy" begs redefinition. The word communism has clearly been defaced, but the word democracy itself has been trashed and mutilated. From the Greek *polis* to the popular uprisings of the Renaissance and Reformation, from the proletarian rebellions that coexisted with the great liberal revolutions, democracy has always been synonymous with the legitimation of power through the people. This legitimation, always concrete, punctual, material, took specific forms, breaking away from a divine or absolute tradition.

With democracy, legitimacy is primarily human, spatially and temporally defined.

We're all subjected to Integrated World Capitalism because it is impossible to locate the source of its power.

If we try to go back to its source, all we find is subjection to the second, third, n^{th} degree.

The origin of power recedes higher and higher up and can be sized up in relation to the depth of our own impotence. Political relationships – called "democratic" – as we experience them on a daily basis, are at best *tropes-l'oeil* when they don't throw us straight into pain and despair. This is the common feature, the unavoidable axiom of the capitalist or socialist restructuration of the political powers.

II. NORTH/SOUTH: TERROR AND HUNGER

As we have begun to see, the capitalist and/or socialist reaction of the 1970s integrates the world market according to a design for the exploitation of work and for political control which evolves in a homogeneous manner. The fundamental transition, in this sense, begins with the phase of Nixonian initiative in the monetary and international political arenas. Between 1971 and 1973, a series of operations lent a political character to the multinational network of exploitation which was already implanted in the world market. The take off of the dollar relative to the gold standard and the petroleum crisis articulated, under the same monetary command, (subtracted from all questions of value) the rules for the organization of work and those of the productive hierarchy on an international level. The petroleum crisis emptied the treasuries of countries and pushed financial centralization and unification to the point of paroxysm. Initially, this operation appeared, during the Kissinger era, as a great shock. The divisions within the capitalist and/ or socialist political personnel reverberated successively in the Trilateral Commission, then through the agreements and the cooptations within Integrated World Capitalism, that is, in the new arrangements of the political will of domination. It is on this foundation that the effective political cartography of exploitation on a world scale is sketched out. Capitalist integration determines certain fundamental polarities around which move dependent subsystems, in partial rupture with the hierarchies of power which overcode the struggles for liberation and the class struggles, that permit capitalist integration to allow itself the luxury, on the level of these subsystems, of large scale modifications. At the heart of this complex play of multicentered systems, which disjoin the flows of struggle and carry out destabilizations and/or strategic stabilizations, a transnational mode of production is consolidated. Throughout these systemic ensembles, one finds the immense enterprise of the production of cybernetic subjectivity [*subjectivité informative*] which regulates the networks of dependence and the processes of marginalization. The working class and the socially productive proletariat of the central metropolitan countries are by virtue of this fact subject to the exponential competition of the proletariat of the large metropolises of underdevelopment. The proletariats of the most developed countries thus are literally terrorized by the spectacle of the extermination by hunger which Integrated World Capitalism imposes on the marginalized (and often limotropic) countries. The industrial reserve army, dominated by a new law of absolute pauperism, is currently constituted on a continental basis. Capitalist and/or socialist command, multiplied into polycentric subaltern subsystems, brings together the highest rates of exploitation with areas of poverty and death. For all that, the struggles for liberation have not been militarily or politically strangled. But, within the frame of these different subsystems, Integrated World Capitalism has not ceased to stimulate fratricidal wars for the conquest of intermediary degrees of participation in integration. The enemy has become the poor, those poorer than oneself. If theory has ever had the need to evaluate the basis of power and of command over human life, it finds in this a convincing example, in that the essence of the problem turns out to be in production and in the organization of work, in the frightening capitalist voraciousness which structures them on a world scale and which subjugates them within the frame of the generalized mass mediated, cybernetic [*informatique*] integration of poles of domination.

To a certain extent, the poor find themselves produced twice by this system: by exploitation and by marginalization and death. Terror, which in the metropolitan countries is incarnated as the potential for nuclear extermination, is actualized, in the marginalized countries, as extermination by famine. Let it be clear, nevertheless, that there is nothing peripheral in this last design: in fact, there are only differences of degree between exploitation, destruction by industrial and urban pollution, welfare conceived as a separating out of zones of poverty, and the extermination of entire peoples, such as those which occur in the continents of Asia, Africa, and Latin America.

It is worth taking proper note the newness of the forms of control implemented by IWC. The strategies of terror and of repression tend to be more and more transversal, punctual, and sudden.

Each piece of earth, each geopolitical segment, has become a potential enemy frontier. The world has been transformed into a labyrinth within which one can fall at any moment, at the will of the destructive options of the multinational powers.

A practice of piracy, corresponding to the current phase of over-maturation of capital, has been substituted for the politics of power of the period of maturity of imperialist capitalism. Flotillas of hyper-power [*sur-puissances*] plow the oceans and the seas the same as Morgan and the Dutch.

We should prepare for the settling of accounts between the submarines of the capitalist and/or socialist nuclear buccaneers. But it is not just in the explicitly military earthly, maritime, and aerial arenas that the permanent war of IWC against world society takes place. It is also in the ensemble of civil, social, economic, and industrial domains. And, there as well, according to infinitely differentiated, transversal filiations of operators of power, who are beyond the control of common humans, beyond union or political control – at least in the traditional sense – and in the middle of which can be found mixed up: multinationals, the Mafias, the military industrial complexes, the secret services, even the Vatican. On all levels, on all scales, everything is permitted: speculation, extortion, provocations, destabilizations, blackmail, massive deportations, genocide… In this virulent phase of decadence, the capitalist mode of production seems to rediscover, intact, the ferociousness of its origins.

All these modalities are inscribed within the same continuum of integration: of information, command, and profit.

If it is true that for a long time, the global struggles of communist liberation will develop – at least in the imagination of revolutionaries – along the East-West axis, one must also acknowledge that the fundamental contradiction which runs through the Integrated Capitalist mode of production today on a world scale is distributed emblematically between the North and the South. If Red Square ever represented a light of hope, the socialist system has currently become the supreme stage of the degeneration of capitalism and is an integral part of the multivalent axis of North-South exploitation. Capitalist and/or socialist restructuring in the 1970s has stitched together the old modes of production, redistributing the functions of the players, and reorganizing on a world scale the division of exploitation.

It is respectable to say, among the western intelligentsia, that, for strategic reasons or for old Maoist memories, the countries of really existing socialism and, in particular the Soviet Union, constitute a greater threat to Europe and the countries of the Third World than the US.

This is not at all our point of view; we do not believe that the West can be preferred to the East. In the sense that we consider ourselves "citizens of the world," we are not concerned with the existing antagonism between the two superpowers. Perilous, debilitating, dramatic – this antagonism is no less in certain regards factitious and mystificatory, in the sense that it is overdetermined by a fundamental functional agreement relative to the subjugation of the productive force of the European proletariats and to the appropriation of a quasi-gratuitous area of expansion and provisioning in raw materials and in labor force on the other continents.

Without calling on, in the last instance, a final Marxist referent, but simply in the light of good sense and of a perception of everyday international relations, it seems to us that the current rise in East-West tension has above all as an object the masking of the destruction by hunger of entire peoples, in an equal fever of reproduction through profit, which torments the dominant castes, as much in the USA as in the USSR. In the long term, therefore: complementarity and complicity in order to assure a common domination on a world scale over the division of labor and its exploitation.

And it is precisely on this scale that the "civilizing mission" of capital has demonstrated the extent of its ferociousness and its absurdity. On that scale, poverty, marginalization, extermination, and genocide are revealed to be the ultimate consequences of a mode of production which set itself up in a till now peaceful symbiosis with the struggles of the working class of the metropolitan countries. But, faced with the crisis of its own system of profit and with the degradation of its own principles of legitimation, capital is now constrained to have recourse (and to theorize that recourse) to the most extreme measures. The era of the over-maturity of capitalism reveals the violence of its origins in a climate of panic due to the weakening of its motivations. The capitalist restructuring of the world market, undertaken since the 1970s, has entailed an extraordinary acceleration of the process of integration, while separating out its effects under the form of paradoxical crises. The capitalist integration of the world market, if it has not crowned the dreams of the promotion of a more humane civilization, has shown, on the contrary, to what level the cruelty and cynicism of the capitalist mode of production can be raised. The attempts to overcome the internal contradictions initiated by the emergence of new collective subjectivities founded on the widening of the market, despite the caution of political personnel of the Kissinger or Carter type, have not only put an end to the internal crisis of the central metropolitan countries, but have pushed it to the point of paroxysm and have spread its devastating effects over the entire globe.

The space dominated by capital, which is subdivided, fragmented, segmented, and functionalized according to the ends of capital's command, is opening as a new terrain of resistance and of conquest. The extreme weapons of extermination and marginalization will not succeed forever in blocking the process of recomposition, whose vitality one can already detect. It is important to underscore the correlation between the level attained by capitalist restructuring and the unprecedented dimensions of the crisis of the past decade. One can thus note, on the one hand, that even in the most terrible of tests, the new social dissidence has not stopped weighing on the situation and accelerating the crisis, and on the other hand, that the capitalist instruments of control are proving to be less and less adapted to their end, more and more ineffective.

It was no doubt beginning in 1982 that the cycle of restructuration, which began between 1971 and 1973, launched a first decisive barrage, when the most indebted countries of the Third World threatened the consortium of banks with the possibility of declaring bankruptcy, in response to the unprecedented politics of deflationary strangulation which they were undergoing. It seems that in an irreversible fashion, a new type of process of liberation and of large scale self-organization came into being. We will return to this point.

III. THE RIGHT IN POWER

The temporal and spatial mechanism for controlling struggles, put in place during the capitalist and/or socialist restructuration of the world of producing, invested new figures of class struggle. In those places where the right triumphed, Integrated World Capitalism succeeded in institutionalizing these new figures and in making them act as a motor of restructuration. As the reactionary cycle of the 1970s puts them on display for us, the instruments set in motion by Integrated World Capitalism in order to channel and even produce class struggle within the frame of institutional integration reside: 1) in its ability to put in place systems of transnational competition between class sectors; 2) in the utilization of deflationary monetary politics which increase unemployment; 3) in the reconversion which it effectuates in the politics of welfare, toward a controlled increase of poverty. This politics is accompanied by a pulverizing, molecular repression of all attempts at resistance and at the free expression of needs. It is essential that the control that it promotes succeeds in becoming effective in the collective imaginary, thus initiating a situation of diffuse crisis within which it will attempt to separate: 1) that part of the proletariat with which incumbent power relies on negotiating a guarantee of reproduction and 2) the immense mass of those excluded or precarious.

This division is multiplied infinitely and hierarchized in the labor market, in which the competition between workers makes itself felt, and beyond, on the "social and institutional market" in which all the other sectors of the population are constrained to "make themselves valuable."

The revolutionary events of 1968, as well as the material transformations of the mode of production, have shown the determining weight which the working class continued to possess on the social stage. The spirit of competition between workers was thus weakened in favor of a recognition of revolutionary objectives concerning a growing number of categories of oppressed people. But with the return of the right to power during the 1970s, a resegregation of the working class, which falls back on already attained advantages, its guarantees, and its corporate privileges, has taken place. We have seen the paradox of an institutionalization which preforms the working class into its own enemy (this time, one can really speak of a "new working class"). In this context, the struggles were condemned to remain institutionalized, to be piloted by Integrated World Capitalism; frequently they even revealed themselves to be the best supports for political and social conservatism. (In particular, on the molecular terrain of capital's subsumption of social work and against the social diffusion of revolutionary needs and transformational desires.) It seems to us essential to insist on this point: today, Stakhanov, the superior dignity of the worker with calloused hands, (for whom Reagan has a certain nostalgia) a certain conception of worker centrality, and the entire old imaginary manipulated by the unions and the left, in a systematic misapprehension of the great majority of the precarious proletariat, has irredeemably gone by the wayside.

"Really existing socialism" has become a privileged

instrument of the division of the metropolitan proletariat, a weapon directly manipulated by capitalist conservatism. Which does not mean, nevertheless, that the working classes, in themselves, can no longer in the future develop decisive struggles within the dynamic of social transformations. But only on the condition that they are radically reshaped by the molecular revolutions which run through them.

In fact, capitalist and/or socialist structuration in the 1970s directly confronted the new revolutionary subjectivities, constraining them to interiorize their potential consciousness and obliging them to be under the thumb of systems of technological control and a battery of government apparatuses which are more and more sophisticated. The fundamental objective of Integrated World Capitalism was to attain a maximal expansion of the integrated productive dimension on the social level and on the geopolitical level, segregated from the reintroduction of poverty, of hunger, and of terror as an instrument of division. The victory of the right was based on its ability to neutralize the recomposition of that revolutionary subjectivity which found itself exposed to the great difficulty of reconstituting unitary lines of attack against exploitation. This reactionary turn around succeeded in assuming, in reversing, and in exploding everything which, since 1968, was revealed as a new power of the proletariat – that is, the ensemble of social components and of collective capacities for articulating the molecular multiplicity of its needs and its desires. The division imposed through instruments of economic and institutional violence was consolidated through the promotion of a symbolism of destruction pushed to an extreme. Exterminism became the referent value par excellence. Extermination by submission or death, as the ultimate horizon of capitalist development. The only law of value which capitalism and/or socialism recognizes today: it is the blackmail of death. We will not let ourselves be taken in by this deathly realism. "It is right to revolt." The responsibility of the traditional organizations of the workers' movement, which remained prisoner to the illusory choice between capitalism and socialism, was thus decisive. It is necessary to recognize that the fact that the development of the mode of production and the maturation of collective consciousness completely passed them by does not in any way eliminate the consequences of their drift, mystification, and paralysis of all initiative in the workers' movement. The inertia of the social movements, which revealed itself in numerous situations, the inability of the revolutionary movement to reconstitute itself on politically new foundations, the incapability of the transformation process to impose itself in its entirety – all are essentially conditioned by the monopoly of political representation and of the imaginary, which the alliance between capitalist and socialist personnel has sealed for decades. This alliance is based on establishing the model of the double labor market: that of guaranteed workers and that of the non-guaranteed – with socialism legitimizing only the first. From this has resulted a frozen society, comparable to that of the *Ancien Régime*, but, in the end, a society equally untenable because it is undermined by innumerable molecular forces expressing its productive essence. This is the source of its nagging thematics of security, of order, and of repression and of its imaginary of urgency, its obsession with crisis, the impression it gives of being able to act only a step at a time, without retreat and without a coherent project. Caught in the same drift, capitalism and socialism now constitute the two pillars of conservatism and in certain cases of quasi-fascist [*fascisante*] reaction.

It is no less true that a new revolution took off in 1968. It is not the fantasms of the "death of the political" or of the "implosion of the social" which will change anything. Beginning in the 1970s, capitalism and/or socialism was constrained to make a parade of its failure on questions of social progress, of the coherent management of economic and social relations on an international scale, of impulsion in the vital domains of technico-scientific creation. It was revealed for what it is, that is, a ferocious and irrational system of repression, which is an obstacle to the development of collective production arrangements and which inhibits the movements of the valorization and capitalization of wealth which it engenders. The world market, far from responding to the principles which liberalism attempts to reestablish, is only an instrument "blocking" for poverty and death, "chaining up" for marginalization and planetary discipline, supported by nuclear terror. We inevitably return to the point: the ultimate "reason" of capitalism and/ or socialism is its impossible tendency toward a sole paradigm: that of a passion to abolish everything which is not in accord with maintaining its power.

But this passion also threatens instrumental reason itself, from inside. In effect, the will towards exclusion and segregation in Integrated World Capitalism tends to turn against itself, by threatening the consistency of its own systems of political communication and reducing to near zero its ability to objectively gauge relations of force. Thus one can beware that before us opens an era of the great paranoiacs of power.

If this is so, the task of reconquering the meaning of work, begun in 1968, is identical to the liberation of life and the reconstitution of reason. For everyone and everywhere: promote the potential carried by the new singularities!

4. THE REVOLUTION CONTINUES

I. RECOMPOSITION OF THE MOVEMENT

In the context of Integral World Capitalism's restructuring of production, undertaken since 1968, the new revolutionary subjectivities are learning to recognize the ruptures imposed by the enemy, to measure their consistency and their effects. The first fundamental determination of Integrated World Capitalism is that, independently of sociological segmentations, it produces a model of subjectivity that is at least tripolar, synchronically cutting across all sorts of unconscious collective levels, personal consciousnesses, and group subjectivities (familial, ethnic, national, racial, etc).

These three poles are: an elitist pole, which comprises both the managerial and technocratic strata of the East and of the West, as well as those of the Third World; a guaranteed pole, cutting across the different specifications of class; and a non-guaranteed pole, which runs through each social stratum equally.

Under these conditions, the new revolutionary subjectivities proclaim, from their point of origin, a desire for peace, collective security, and minimal safeguards against unemployment and poverty. One finds a fear of the hell of the absence of guarantees at the heart of the three poles of subjectivity: among entirely deprived groups, among proletarian groups already somewhat guaranteed by wage labor and welfare, as well as among certain sectors of the elite whose status is made systematically precarious. Thus the essential basis of contemporary production is constituted by this fluctuating mass and continuous mixture of guarantism and precariousness. The precarious constitute a fundamental point of support for the constitution of capitalist power: it is in terms of them that the institutions of repression and marginalization find their consistency. But in counterpoint, they assume a social role within the new framework of power and exploitation, because of the values and productive potential of which they are the bearers. They are also focal points of imagination and struggle which are capable of catalyzing singular becomings, of bringing to light other references, other praxes, appropriate for breaking the immense machine of discipline and control of the collective force of production.

The history of the struggles of the 1970s has already sketched the process of recomposition and of social liberation. A number of matrices of rupture were opened then by the new proletarian movements. Whatever their diversity, they all originated in the tremendous mutations of an increasingly complex, overpowering, and deterritorializing social productive force, and they all affirm themselves with reinforced clarity against the repressive normalization and restructuration brought about by social segmentation and stratification. These phases of struggle were most significant for workers as an experience of discovery and comprehension of the cesuras and corporatist overcodings imposed on the proletarian socius, and as an experience of internal struggle against the violence by which Integrated World Capitalism has constantly tried to interdict processes of innovation wherever they are involved. Internal struggles thus recuperate the tripolar segmentation of Integrated World Capitalism within the struggles of each subjective component. Since this always occurs at each phase in the emergence of a new social subjectivity, their quality, force, and cohesion is self-composed [*auto-agencée*], the result of a collective self-making. Need, consciousness, and production are fused at the heart of such a process. The 1970s were thus marked by the continuous emergence of moments of rupture punctuating the capitalist and/or socialist attempts at restructuration, all of which are characterized by new subjective problematics and by a special collective effort to redefine their perspective.

From 1977 in Italy to the "Great Break" in Central Europe (Germany, Switzerland, Holland), from the Iranian revolution to the period of Solidarity, to the renewal of revolutionary struggles in Central America, to the enormously important liberation movements that are beginning to erupt in the Southern Cone... wherever we turn, we find these principle characteristics of the project. The struggles that are internal and antagonistic to the politics of reactionary restructuration are mobilizing, either against their repressive texture, or inside these processes of subjective development as a unifying tension and as a self-liberating perspective. Revolutionary struggles have never "targeted" to this extent the theoretical definition and the practical realization of an orientation resting intrinsically on collective subjectivation and implying, in consequence, the destruction of all ideologies of an external vanguard. Autonomy has never appeared with more force as a primary objective. We repeat: there is nothing anarchic about this, since it essentially has to do with a qualitative autonomy, capable of apprehending the social complexity of movements, and of grasping it as a process of subjective convergence, centered on the quality of life and on the communitarian restructuring of production goals, and since it is equally a matter, by virtue of this reconstruction, of assuming peace against all forms of terrorism and of imposing mass negotiation as a basis of mobilization and of organization.

It is obviously necessary to be very careful when we broach the question of the experiences and the initiatives of the new subjects. Frequently, during the course of the events we have just evoked (from 1977 in Italy forward), the action of these new subjects has been presented, from a theoretical point of view, as a hypostasis and, from a practical point of view, as a linear function. Once again, one risked falling into the old mythology of mass action. This has to do with illusions that probably inevitably result from deception and regression. But it would be difficult to determine the stakes of the theoretical elucidation of this question. The theoretical struggle against such illusions leads to patient acceptance, without reservation, of the real situation, that is, of the fact that the universality of the proposition of transformation must necessarily be diluted in the multiplicity of movements, the contradictory moments which characterize them and in the long term of the movement of collective imagination.

Before developing this point, we must first insist on the constructive effort that the new modes of subjectivation have already accomplished on a stage profoundly changed in relation to the history and the traditions of the revolutionary and workers' movements, because of expanded competency and performance in the arrangements of subjectivity at work on that stage. Confronted by the amplitude of the production of totalitarian subjectivity by the capitalist states, the revolutionary arrangements pose the problem of the quality of life, of reappropriation, and of self-production in an equally sizable dimension. Through a movement with multiple heads and a proliferating organization, their episodes of liberation will be capable of investing the entire spectrum of production and reproduction.

Each molecular movement, each autonomy, each minoritarian movement will coalesce with an aspect of the real in order to exalt its particular liberatory dimensions. It will thus break with the schema of exploitation that capital imposes as the dominant reality. It is this new consciousness of the modern proletariat – deterritorialized and fluctuating – which will permit envisaging the rupture of capitalist segmentation and the reformulation not of commands, not of programs, but of diagrammatic propositions of communism and of liberation And it is capitalist restructuration's hyper-reactionary character that explains the positively catastrophic acceleration which the movement has experienced since the beginning of the 1980s. Nonetheless this restructuration has not damaged the emerging points of new proletarian subjectivities; it has simply reduced their elasticity. Numerous signs indicate to us that once again the movement is on the verge of stepping forward to undo the repressive obstructions which have successfully blocked its force during this last period.

If we return to the tripartition proposed earlier and if we examine how the process of recomposition runs through the elitist pole, the guaranteed pole, and the non-guaranteed pole, we can discover the forcefulness with which the movement of new alliances has posed its premises. This is immediately evident once one takes into account the fluidity of relations that the crisis has introduced and continues to accentuate between the guaranteed and the non-guaranteed sectors. But this is no less evident when one considers the articulations which the elitist pole has with the two others. Many individuals who evolve in management and at the highest levels of the institutions of knowledge were, during the past ten years, not only implicated in the process of precarization that is coterminal with their role and function, but also introduced to an elaborated critical consciousness regarding the legitimacy of their status. The irrationality and the madness of the extended reproduction choices of IWC, the obsession of the arms race and of nuclear war, the vertigo of famine and genocide which deepen the differences and engender cleavages, to the point of pushing certain managerial elites to the point of refusal and dissidence. This process, which is all too frequently disfigured and made ridiculous when it is reported in a propagandistic way, nonetheless demonstrates the expansion of resistance in the new forms of subjectivity. Previously, one of the slogans of the communists was the proposed importation of the class struggle into the institutions: today we note more modestly that the new subjects are capable of exporting their values and their antagonistic recommendations to the highest levels of management and of the institutions of knowledge. The true processes of dissidence are not recuperable; it is not a commodity that can be sent to the enemy as a gift.

In point of fact, the revolution continues. The

irreversible character of the hitherto completed processes affirms itself. The new subjectivities rearrange their political identity by assimilating (that is, semiotizing and smothering) the obstacles posed by the adversary – including those that the adversary has made them introject. The changing characteristics of the collective force of labor, the living forces of the precarious urban proletariat, the transfinite network of dissident discursive arrangements set themselves up as so many protagonists of the new cycle of struggle.

II. THE TERRORIST INTERLUDE

The development of new subjectivities has undergone deep internal breaks during the course of this process which result primarily from the capitalist mode of production that we have just described and from the internal convulsions of the movements.

Each historical period can be affected by the birth of elitist poles and by extremist surges of self-exaltation which develop to the detriment of the interests of the movements whose interests they pretend to represent. That was particularly evident during this period when Integrated World Capitalism worked to defend and reconstitute the model of a systematic segmentation of both social movements and ideologies.

Terrorism was perhaps the deepest and maddest cesura that revolutionaries experienced during the entire course of the 1970s. In the face of reactionary pressure exercised by the state and by IWC to block the liberation movement, faced by attempts to divide and force competition between different exploited groups in order to freeze constitutional and social relations at regressive levels, and faced with the deathly rigidity of the dominant power's formations, whole sectors of the movement were seized by rage and frustration. In the context of the molecular effervescence and maturation of new revolutionary subjectivities, the state has an interest in imposing a molar order of return to a reinforced social dichotomy; it thus undertakes to make a parade of its power by adopting drastic measures and in deploying highly sophisticated mechanisms of control and repression. For the same occasion, state terrorism undertakes to destroy without distinction all political and existential dissidence.

On this terrain, IWC has carried out a veritable mobilization of state functions and set going a new type of civil war: not only by military and police means and by states of emergency, but also by means of a psychological and informational war and by corresponding cultural and political strategies.

During the 1970s, this sort of civil war created a favorable basis for the development of the most extreme reaction. In order to understand what happened then, it is necessary to bear in mind the sizable stakes of the contest of force between, on the one hand, the new desires and needs of the collective subjectivity, and on the other hand, the different components working for the restoration and restructuration of production and command. It is true that the civil war frequently gave the State the chance to give itself powers and the instigation to react against a situation that it no longer controlled. The new revolutionary movements also have everything to gain from clearly recognizing the realities within which they operate. All the more so because certain groups can have the illusion of having some measure of control by their own means over this sort of situation, by taking the risk of placing themselves on the molar terrain of confrontation hoped for by the enemy, by identifying in some sense with him, by entering fully into the imaginary traps of political domination which are dangled in front of the movement.

The 1970s were thus years of a civil war whose direction, imposed by IWC, led to pure and simple exterminations, like those of the Palestinians. One cannot deny that within this context, a terrorism of worker and proletarian origins sometimes managed to take the initiative, but nevertheless without ever stepping out of that vicious circle of capitalist overdetermination. Rather than reducing that overdetermination, such terrorism only reinforced the will of the dominant powers to isolate, to make examples of, and to neutralize the conflicts.

The perspective of the revolutionary movement, in correspondence with real historical transformations, manifests itself altogether differently. How will the new subjective components be able to conquer supplementary spaces of life and liberty? How, by illuminating other types of force, intelligence, and sensibility, can the power of the enemy be deprived of its substance? These, more appropriately, are the questions of the revolutionary movement.

From all points of view, red terrorism was a disastrous interlude for the movement But especially for the way it relaunched ideological and abstract centralist conceptions of organization. Its crazy search for central points of confrontation became redundant with an ossified Leninism, which is disconnected from all historical materiality, reduced entirely to a statist interpretation, a sort of paranoid point of reference which it sought to impose on the recomposition of the movement. Nothing is more urgent than to have done with this false alternative. Access to the movement must be denied to these absurd messengers of the past. Red terrorism has only one end: that of failure and despair. It has only one function: to stem the immense liberatory potential which has revealed itself at the heart of this heavy period of reaction through which we are going. In as much as it complied with the rhythms of history and with the programmings of the opponent, red terrorism has revealed itself for what it is: a paradoxical form of conservatism.

But haven't the capitalist formations of power on the same occasion taken the measure of the autonomous movements and secreted antibodies capable of robbing them of power? It is precisely this question which confronts the militants of prior generations who reemerge, as from a fog, from the great reactionary disaster.

The terrorist interlude of proletarian origin in the 1970s has become exceedingly, mortally dangerous for the progress of those revolutionary processes which had begun to de-totalize, to deterritorialize the stratifications of power, at all levels. Clearly, the ideologies that nurtured it should be forcefully avoided as so many biases which can only adulterate the struggles of the real movement and lead them to defeat. Given this, it is necessary to recognize that this terrorist wave posed a real problem through radically false premises and responses: how can the resistance to reaction be linked to a new type of organization? The correct response to this question, and the strategic line which follows from it, are already in the movement, at those points where it constitutes itself through an institutional mode without going astray on the paths of statist legitimation. It has to do with constructing a new society, a new politics, a new womens' movement, an other workers' movement, other youth movements. "Other," "different," "new" – always the same feeble words to index the vectors of happiness and imagination which are capable of overthrowing the sclerotic world where politics is nothing but frustration and paranoia, where society is nothing but the triumph of conformism, where the workers' movement gets bogged down in corporatism, the womens' movement in the introjection of subordination, the youth movement in all sorts of drugs, and where, finally, the limit between the demand for power and terrorism continues to be confining.

It is equally possible that the external cesura was the symptom of an internal illness. It would be absurd to deny that the processes of recomposition also carry dogmatic and sectarian elements, viruses from old stratifications which threaten them from inside. It is thus the articulation between immediacy and mediation, tactics and strategy – which can only be established by way of multilateral and practical relations – which risks running headlong into chaos, maniacal agitation, and provocation. And if it has been so, then the only possible way to heal this kind of paranoia is to be found by the revelation and exaltation of its symptoms, the exploration of its etiology, the disengaging of the desires of which it is the expression and their radical liberation from all overcodings by the capitalist death drives.

The problem of the recourse to force has not for all this

disappeared from our horizon. But we consider it to be all the more politically efficacious if the forces in question are diversified, multiplied by a thousand links to thought and the imagination. Force is the body – and we want to reconstruct the movement outside the dead body which tradition has left us; we want to reinvent a living, real body, to live and to experience a physiology of collective liberation. It is on death to life, from the destruction of being to the construction of the world. At this phase of the movement and of historical development, it seems to us that only a continuous and multidimensional revolution can constitute an alternative to the failed projects of archeo-socialism. This obviously does not entail holding to general considerations. Each singular component of the movement develops systems of value which should be considered in themselves, without requiring either translation or interpretation. These systems are permitted to evolve in their own appropriate directions and to exist at times in contradictory relationships with each other. They don't participate any the less in the same project of constructing a new type of social reality.

In the 1970s, a first experiment at bringing together the revolutionary processes began on a positive terrain: that of the anti-nuclear and ecology movements. They were immediately linked and implicated in alternative programs for the recovery of productive energy. Thus, ecology was not trapped by nostalgia or by protest; it demonstrated that a new style of action was possible. Moreover, the anti-nuclear struggles opened specific horizons in terms of the exploitation and accumulation of the scientific labor force. The struggles of technical and scientific workers, which will be revealed as essential to the development of the communist program, are beginning to illuminate the complex dimensions of an alternative use of science. Moreover, it is at the point of articulation between this use and the collective force of production that the decisive mutation of the communist project will occur. It is on the same continuum of struggles against exploitation and for positive alternatives that, more and more, the capitalist and/or socialist exploitation of time will be put in question and that a new type of communitarian organization of the productive forces will begin. Struggles against the labor process and its overcoding of time; struggles for alternative housing arrangements and for another way of conceptualizing domestic sociality, neighborliness, and cooperation between segments of the socius.

This has to do with positively conjugating the critique of science and the struggle against exploitation, for example, to conjugate research on alternative energy sources and the practical reconstruction of the productive community. It is only at this price that we will succeed in grasping the coherence of the current proletarian projects through the multiplicity and diversity of the initiatives which actualize those projects and the wealth of their productive end. We take for granted, the fact that the destruction of property, as the fundamental juridical form of capitalist accumulation, and the destruction of bureaucratic control, as the fundamental juridical form of socialist accumulation, in one indissociable intertwining in which they present themselves today for analysis, constitute the essential conditions for the liberation of science and the elaboration of an open and communitarian social life and for the development of diffuse and creative forms of organization of social work which correspond to the new proletarian subjectivities. What we are evoking here is not a utopia. It is the explication of a real movement, which innumerable traces and indices designate as a power in action.

The elaboration of the political economy of this transition has become an urgent problem; the communist program will broach a new level of consciousness only to the extent that it makes advances regarding these questions. In terms of this, it goes without saying that the specific programs of the different movements cannot help but become intertwined. It is the same regarding their passage to organizational form, by way of diverse attempts of a highly spontaneous character. A priority in this domain is the positivity of perspectives which forbid lapsing into Jacobinism or

Leninism. We must insist again on the materiality of these passages, on the manner in which they succeed in demonstrating their force, even in the worst sectors of capitalist reaction, and how they succeed in planting in the very marrow of the bosses and the bureaucrats the thorn of their changing perspective.

We have already invoked a major illustration of this conjunction of radically heterogeneous vectors for overcoming the worst plans of the reactionary employers: that of the international monetary system. In the summer of 1982, the declaration of non-payment of debts and the threat of bankruptcy among the large Latin American countries struck a perhaps fatal blow against Reaganomics. The internal resistance of the working classes in the developed countries to unemployment and inflation thus found itself objectively associated with the suppression of the proletariats of the Third World, themselves undermined by poverty and famine. The objective character of this new de facto alliance, its considerable political incidences, does not indicate to us the historical limits of reaction: they confirm the potential for intervention in collective arrangements of subjectivity, when they succeed in joining their interventions along the fault line of the crisis. For twelve years after 1971, from Nixon to Reagan, big multinational capital succeeded in instituting a perfidious mechanism for augmenting productivity within the framework of a general immobilization of the relations of force and of the distribution of incomes – in 1982, it was the very bases of capitalist power which were put in question, as a result of the conjoined resistance of the diverse sectors of the international proletariat. One must admit that during this long period of historical latency, the collective subjectivity had to continue to metabolize its needs and its desires. If not, how could such a crisis have been possible – the first in the present historical cycle of reaction, but of a striking conspicuousness. This is a clear example of what we mean when we speak of the "materiality of the passageways of the recomposition of subjectivity."

Parallel to a growing consciousness of the irreversible

character of the crisis of the capitalist mode of production arises a fundamental problem: capitalism and/or socialism control the means of destroying the world; will they use these means to defend their domination? And to what point? Now, it is precisely around this threat that the recomposition of revolutionary subjectivities and the development of movements has partially reconstructed its highest profile. It is in the struggles for peace that the movement attains its richest and most complex expression. In a sinuous and continuous fashion, the struggles are carried out across the enemy territory, preventing him from attaining the maximum concentration of the destructive force that defines his project and, in a continuous way, from attaining his force of persuasion and concentration. One could almost say that this "guerrilla of peace," which is taking root in the spaces between individual consciousnesses, constructed on a communitarian basis, collectively synchronizing the dispositions and sequences of the domination which constitutes them in terms of resistance and struggle, all of this is already a force, a project, which makes us relinquish the defensive, which surpasses the war of position and which can inspire us to a war of movement. What other method is there for struggling for peace than to encircle, to empty the enemy strategies of their substance, to destructure them from inside? In this regard, is it necessary to distinguish the advancement of the pacifist struggle from that of recomposing the projects of revolutionary action? Not at all, because, we repeat, the struggle for peace carries within it the highest possible alternative potentialities.

We hope no one will think us so naive as to imagine that there are not as many scoundrels as honest people under the mantle of pacifism. In certain countries, the peace movement is instrumentalized and perverted by methods which recall to us those abject times of the "Stalinist peace." Neither are we taken by a "peace" of social neutralization which would accommodate, for example, the muzzling of the Polish people. On the contrary, we conceive the struggle for peace as a loom on which the collective struggles for liberation can be woven. That is, for us, the struggle is not synonymous with the status quo. It has to do fundamentally, therefore, with lifting that hypothesis of the overdetermination of death which weighs down all the capitalist and/or socialist relations of production. The struggle for peace is a struggle for a democracy in which the liberty of individuals would be guaranteed and in which the question of the res publica and of the goals of economic development would find their legitimation in the community. Green is born neither from the red of the socialist regimes nor from the black of the capitalist regimes. It is born from refusing poverty and of oppression wherever it proliferates and from the urgent desire to be freed from the fear of capitalist control wherever it is imposed. Everyone tells us: "You should choose sides." Some tell the Afghans that they would be occupied by the Americans if the Russians left. But would that be worse? "If the Americans occupy us," those involved respond, "we will all become Scythians." Others tell us we would be occupied by the Russians if we refuse the American umbrella. But would that be worse? If the Russians occupy our country we will all become Poles. We have had enough of all of this blackmail. We similarly reject the blackmail of the bomb as well as the supposed values of capitalism or socialism.

Peace is a pre-condition of revolution.

Within the tragedy which capital imposes on life, a collective response is sketched: in the shadow of destruction, an ethical exigency of happiness and of life is affirmed. The mobilization for peace opens up infinite routes for liberation; the constructive forms in which liberty is today draped can alone dissolve the power of death behind which the capitalist classes are retrenching. Yes, the revolution continues: the reactionary wave of the 1970s has not destroyed it. It has enriched itself by a sort of irreversible strategic interiorization which permits it to be intrinsically articulated with the immense ethical project for peace.

5. THE NEW ALLIANCE

I. A MOLECULAR METHOD OF AGGREGATION

The transformations which trouble a society require a new type of organization. Leninism or anarchism are no longer anything today but phantasms of defeat, voluntarism, and disenchantment, a forced faith or solitary rebellion, an antithetical form of repression or a simple abstract assertion of singularity. The organizational choices of the future movement should be rethought independently of the ideological and political references to the traditional workers' movement which led that movement to defeat. The collapse of the two extreme models – Leninism and anarchism – leave altogether open the question of the machines of struggle which the movement must make use of in order to be capable of winning. Their multifunctional and uniquely characterized articulation of the singularities which constitute them imply that the form of these machines no longer repeats the centralist project and no longer retains the illusion of filtering democracy through centralist structures. One always finds in pseudo-democratic centralism a traced copy of statist models. In it, the repressive and bureaucratic characteristics of the state of Richelieu, Robespierre, and Rothschild are replayed and illusorily reversed. For too long, the revolutionary movement has, through passivity or refusal, been subject to this homology. How can the state be destroyed by an organism which puts up with hegemony, even on a formal level? But how can such a task be made a primary concern of an "other" movement, a different one which is founded on the self-valorization and the self-production of singularities?

Obviously, we have no model of organizational replacement, but at least we know what we no longer want. We refuse everything which repeats the constitutive models of representative alienation and the rupture between the levels where political will is formed and the levels of its execution and administration. As always happens, in the real course of a revolutionary process, the new organizational "proposals" correspond to the new essence of the social productive force. And they are its fluidity, the multivalence of its conceptual references, its permanent capacity of abstraction, its pragmatic efficiency, and its power to deterritorialize undermining every attempt to divide and stratify the forces inside the organizational process. The formation, execution and administration of political direction should no longer be separated, because that constitutes a repression of the collective labor force's new characteristics. The time of Montesquieu and the separation of powers is over. The alienated relationships developed by pseudo-democratic centralism on the executive and administrative levels, regardless of how it presents itself, are in the process of disappearing from the political horizon of the revolution (from which Rousseau and the notion of the alienation of individual wills shall also be removed).

But, up to this point, our attempt at redefinition has only progressed negatively: more positively, what signifies the organization of revolutionary subjectivity?

Let's advance a step at a time and try to better answer the question.

The supposedly "definitive" argument of those who uphold the traditional models of organization consists in affirming that only one centralized form can prove sufficiently efficacious in constituting general fronts of struggle; that is all the more true in capitalism's current phase of development, and this would imply as well an excess of centralizing force in the organization of the oppressed.

All of this is rather stupid. It would only be true if society's current submission to capital was dependent on a rule relating accumulated value to the quantity of exploitation and if a specific form of command were necessarily associated with a particular kind of social production. But isn't this precisely the sort of measure and the type of relationship that we have left behind? The generalization of capitalist exploitation is visibly accompanied by a change in the nature of the repressive functions, such that every structural regulation tends to be eliminated. Properly speaking, there is no longer value to be reappropriated. If the law of value continued to function, at a level of abstract generality, one could perhaps once again conceive of Leninist type organizational projects. But there is no such thing. Capitalist command is presently developing in direct and antagonistic engagement with the free and proliferating singularities. Whatever rigid and repressive nets it throws after this wild faun, it will not succeed in reaching or catching either its mode of temporalization or its essential riches and goals.

Given these conditions, the task of organizing new proletarian forms must be concerned with a plurality of relations within a multiplicity of singularities – a plurality focused on collective functions and objectives that escape bureaucratic control and overcoding, in the sense that the plurality develops towards optimizing the processes of involved singularities. What is at stake here then is a functional multicentrism capable, on the one hand, of articulating the different dimensions of mass intellectuality, and on the other hand of actively neutralizing the destructive power of capitalist arrangements. This is the first positive characteristic of the new revolutionary subjectivity. Its cooperative, plural, anti-centralist, anti-corporatist, anti-racist, anti-sexist dimensions further the productive capacities of the singularities. Only qualified in this way will proletarian struggles be able to reconstitute coherent and effective fronts of struggle. These organizational processes should be conceived as being essentially dynamic: each singularity is given impetus by objectives which are not only local but which themselves expand more and more until they begin to define points of transsectoral contact nationally and internationally.

Global projects of society, based in closed ideologies, thus lose all relevance, all operative ability. It is no longer a matter of being founded in abstract syntheses, but in open processes of analysis, critique, verification, and concrete, singular realization. From a molecular point of view, each attempt at ideological unification is an absurd and indeed reactionary operation. Desire, on a social terrain, refuses to allow itself to be confined to zones of consensus, in the arenas of ideological legitimation. Why ask a feminist movement to come to a doctrinal or programmatic accord with ecological movement groups or with a communitarian experiment by people of color or with a workers' movement, etc.? Ideology shatters; it only unifies on the level of appearance. On the contrary, what is essential is that each movement shows itself to be capable of unleashing irreversible molecular revolutions and of linking itself to either limited or unlimited molar struggles (and only collective analysis and critique can decide which) on the political and syndical terrain of defending the general rights of the national and/or international community…

The invention and construction of these new organizational schemas imply the creation of permanent mechanisms for analyzing the internal goals of the social subjectivity's own processes of self-production. This is the sine qua non for guaranteeing a real questioning of the modes of collective functioning and for preventing the emergence of sectarian tendencies.

This seems to us to be the positive starting-point of a revolutionary method of organization adequate to the collective subjectivity bearing it: a scientific method in its mode of analysis, yet open to historical processes and capable of imagination. "Work in progress" in the chain links of singularities, all oriented toward their self-production and multiplication. A method, therefore, which is constitutive of an organization which continually remakes itself, a method thereby conjoined to the productive forces which have made the singularities and their development the basis of material and spiritual wealth.

II. MACHINES OF STRUGGLE

The analysis has progressed; experience has accumulated. The method has already been given some verification. Is it possible to rethink and begin to realize the organizational forms of this new revolutionary subjectivity? To pose this question already implies a confrontation with the difficulties, the material modalities, the obstacles, the enemies of the collective liberation project. How to conceive the composition and reconstruction of the movements? How to rebegin developing each of them in their extensive articulations? We find ourselves faced with numerous, heterogeneous topics and with fluctuating options – the different organized structures of the movement are not only jealous of their singularity, but they seem sometimes to open themselves only for defensive struggles, for the reinforcement and the permanent affirmation of that singularity. In addition, their logics are presented according to changing and multiple matrices; they're always rearticulating the rhizome of their different autonomous components in a different way. It goes without saying that the problem of ideological agreement or disagreement is no longer posed here in terms of the usual political logic – neither one belongs to the same ideological universe. On the contrary, the first problem to be resolved is arranging for the coexistence of multiple ideological dimensions and developing an analysis and a confrontation which, without trying to overcome specific differences, nevertheless tries to prevent them from degenerating into passive and mute divisions. We therefore imagine a process of recomposition which takes for granted conflictual variations within the dynamics of singularization, respecting each's wealth and responsibility for carrying human productivity.

That said, it is nonetheless necessary to construct machines of struggle, organizational devices which are open to these dynamics and to this functional multicentrism.

These machines of struggle will be all the more effective in that their field of action will be limited and in that they will establish for themselves the fundamental goal of perfecting the singularization processes.

Such modes of organizational crystallization appeared in North America in the 1960s, at the time of the different campaigns of the movement. The same thing in Germany in the 1970s, where the development of the alternative movement revealed the existence of lines of differentiation going in the direction of both maximizing singularization and in materially recomposing the possibilities of struggle. An open method, therefore, that takes substance from its openness to engender an open organization.

It frequently happens – as much in Arab, Slavic, Latin American as in Anglo-Saxon countries – that this experimentation with new forms of organization develops from within a religious imaginary. Undoubtedly, one must distinguish between religious motivations which attach to an act of liberation and those which are reterritorialized around theological alienation.

It is a fact that in a world whose sole "burrs" can only be non-significant ruptures, the reconquest of the value of witness, of personal engagement, of singular resistance, and of basic solidarity has become an essential motor of transformation. In order to constitute a machine of struggle, the movements are obliged to assume, as completely as possible, a contradictory relation between singularity and capitalist society, between ethics and politics. And this is scarcely conceivable except on the condition that the forms of militancy are totally reinvented. We should lead the analysis and critique of militancy and of previous experiences, when they make us sad, when they become historically tarnished, because they constitute obstacles to a liberating praxis. But it strikes us as impossible that a new open method of organization could be founded without concretely redefining a new militancy – whatever the breadth of its motivations. That is, a certain social crystallization of desire and of generosity runs through all singularities.

One can expect from this way of conceiving things not only the birth of new organizations, changed machines of struggle, but equally a profound modification of their propositional context, in particular a redefinition of the "Rights of Man" guaranteeing and encouraging communitarian constructions. Generally speaking, this entails a renewal of constitutional mechanisms and of their capacity to register the conflicts and social changes which will be posed.

Only that subjectivity engaged in the singular processes of production can break the codes and norms of the production of subjectivity of IWC It is only on this path that democracy can be reestablished. Juridical innovation necessarily takes place via the institutionalization of the real movement. The only acceptable juridical norm – corresponding in other words to the "instances of justice" inscribed in groups of people themselves – is the image-movement of the real. Inversely, IWC presents us with societies in which rights are overthrown and in which the legal codes and constitutions are either put aside, or function as simple umbrellas for illegal practices on the part of castes acting in their own interest.

Taking charge of these constitutional problematics should no longer be overlooked and abandoned, as was the case in the movement for a long time, but belongs properly to the revolutionary orchestrations of political will. It is the relation between political will and the constitution of the state which is inverted here. It will be for the first to condition the second, not the reverse, as conservative ideologues suggest and as reactionary practices impose. This reversal does not imply renouncing the existence of a coherent juridical tradition. On the contrary, it derives from the will to promote in that tradition a higher rationality, a greater care for truth and justice, by integrating within its mechanisms a capacity for reading the essential mutational processes. In sum, the "spirit of the laws" must acquire a sharp sensibility and intelligence regarding the profound progressive transformations of the social "market."

It is interesting to note that the recent apologists of the market and its miracle-working power are outraged opponents of any promotion of this kind of market.

The fact is that at the current level of the capitalist crisis and the relations of force between the classes, such political and institutional free market devices, by facilitating and inciting collective liberty's potential, would destroy, even annul the conditions of the liberal-bourgeois market of exploitation. It is thus clear that, while we contest the state's pretensions to lord over social conflict in a contractual manner (a practice which is invariably a source of totalitarianism), we do not for all that speak for those falsely naive attempts to seize the processes of social singularization, only pretending to acknowledge them under the aegis of a corporate project (which they try then to integrate into what is pompously called the "social economy." The pseudo-Proudhonian ideology cloaking certain of these attempts has no other goal than to render them captive to an expanded capitalist market.) Corporatism, however it presents itself, should be overturned; it can only generate ersatz, false solutions to the problematics of new subjectivities. All statist manipulations, the ingratiating as well as the disgraceful, must be relentlessly combated. Statism and corporatism are two faces of the same obstacle to the development of autonomies and of singularities. We repeat: the machines of struggle, carried by new proletarian subjectivities, tend to essentially deepen the singularity of the collective situation from which they emanate, without in any way damaging their oppositional, revolutionary relation with the state.

This is only a paradox if one misapprehends the movement's liberating goals and, especially, the interest of each of its components in the disappearance of techniques of power and group manipulations inherent in traditional systems of representation "in the name of," supposedly, the general will. We have had our account of Menenius Agrippa and his apologists! Thus the machines of struggle will develop their productive activities and political action in direct contact with, and the same texture as the distinct contexts within which they are formed. They will engage in production and reproduction simultaneously. Within production, in order to prepare society's capacity for autonomous and communist management of human activities, and in order to construct a new type of economy founded on collective arrangements which connect different modalities of semiotic and machinic practice. And, within the whole of society, in order to set up the reproduction and organization of the distribution and functions of work time, self-managed and as-free-as-possible. Thus, a promotion of the collective as much as of initiative, of creation and of individual responsibility. As we know, the neoliberal sycophants love to return to the mythologies of the boss, as the sole guarantor of the rational ordering of complex productive processes, as the only possible agent of the dynamization of the force of labor, etc.... At the same time, they try to discredit self-management as being synonymous with mediocracy, (impossible to apply on a large scale, etc.). All their reasoning proceeds from a total misapprehension of the means of collective semiotization which are now at work in all the significant arenas of science and technology. A certain conception of treelike hierarchies and oppressive disciplines has undoubtedly become passé. It no longer has to do with a simple question of taste or of democratic prejudice. The extensive arrangement, in rhizome, of machinic components, of informational components, and of decision-making components has become an absolute necessity, if production is to keep up, to further society, science, art, in sum, human life on this planet. After a few centuries of socialist and/or capitalist domination, production and society have become one and the same thing. There is no turning back from this fact. Machines of revolutionary struggle are themselves obliged to become disposed for producing new social realities and new subjectivities.

We emphasize again that the definition, the general program of this multidimensional liberation does not belong to these machines of struggle; it belongs to the rhizomatic multiplicity of singularity processes, within each of their production sites, which they transform, remaking and, should the case arise, multiplying the power that this liberation authorizes.

From now on, organizing signifies first: work on oneself, in as much as one is a collective singularity; construct and in a permanent way reconstruct this collectivity in a multivalent liberation project. Not in reference to a directing ideology, but within the articulations of the real. Perpetually recomposing subjectivity and praxis is only conceivable in the totally free movement of each of its components, and in absolute respect of their own times – time for comprehending or refusing to comprehend, time to be unified or to be autonomous, time of identification or of the most exacerbated differences.

Liberation, production, the constitution of new social arrangements, all arise from distinct levels – equally important – on the basis of which the machines of struggle develop. The experiences of community and solidarity seen by the second half of this century illuminate the original paradigms of those new organizations which we call machines of struggle. It's necessary now to deploy their free play and their power. It is clear that only the direct experience of struggle will determine their contour – to try to describe in advance what the machines of struggle of new proletarian subjectivities will be on a practical level (of desire and cognition) would run contrary to their essential mode, which depends on what one no longer dares to call "the masses."

III. TODAY, NEW LINES OF ALLIANCE

At the end of a period of defensive retrenchment – the result of the current repressive wave under the aegis of capitalist and/or socialist organization – a special form of alliance can and must be realized between the constitutive categories of the new proletariat and the most dynamic sectors of productive society. Distinguishing this alliance is, first, that it can break the corporatist obstacles to restructuring, which have shown themselves to be particularly effective amongst the industrial working classes as well as in the tertiary service and scientific sectors of social production. The basic revolutionary sequence presently confronting us concerns the possibilities of making the working classes, the tertiary production sectors, and those innumerable components of the universe of the precarious connect and interact. The movement will have to take up this problematic of conjunction with all of their intelligence and energy. Not because the working class would remain the determining element of the revolutionary process. Neither that the tertiary, intellectual, marginal, etc. sectors would be the bearers of essential economic changes. There's nothing to gain from entertaining such historic misunderstandings. It is clear that the discourses on workers' centrality and hegemony are thoroughly defunct and that they cannot serve as a basis for the organization of new political and productive alliances, or even simply as a point of reference. Breaking with this sort of trap, the true question concerns the invention of a system, not of unification, but of multivalent engagement of all social forces which are not only in the process of articulating new subjective forces, but also of breaking the blocks of capitalist power – in particular their powers of mass media suggestion on a considerable portion of the oppressed.

It would be fictive and artificial to expect to find these new affiliations only at ruptures in the structure, in areas of friction in the labor market and the corporatist reorganization of different segments of the working class. Such an attitude would still be part of the spirit of IWC, which is always more ready to apply repression than to consider attempts to liberate production. Now, we have seen that the question of recomposing the movement's conjunctive unity goes hand in hand with that of the self-production of emancipation – at once intrinsically singular and externally offensive in their tendency – by each of its components. Now self-production implies effective and unreserved recognition of everything that really participates in new types of cooperation and subjectivity, unalloyed with the dominant power formations. The new anticapitalist alliance will destroy the corporatist chains of repression and help replace their viewpoint with those of a collective self-transformation.

Instead of new political alliances, we could say just as well: new productive cooperation.

One always returns to the same point, that of production – production of useful goods, production of communication and of social solidarity, production of aesthetic universes, production of freedom...

The fact is that the center of gravity of these productive processes has been displaced toward the molecular web of marginal and minority concerns. Nevertheless, it's not a matter of founding a new religion and creating point by point oppositions between the whole group of guaranteed workers and the precarious workers. On the contrary, it has to do with finishing with the latter representing themselves as a heterogeneous ensemble, excluded in essence from the "true realities" of production, as all the representational coordinates of capitalism and/or socialism beguile them into thinking... Yet such a transformation implies as well that numerous sectors of the working class and the privileged categories of the productive proletariats give themselves other "representations" than those which they possess today and which, for the most part, are part of the corporatist regime. The molecular revolutions, the new subjective arrangements, autonomies and processes of singularization are capable of restoring a revolutionary meaning to the struggles of the working class and indeed many sectors of the collective force of labor, which are now reduced to vegetating in their sociological stratifications. We believe that the proletarian recomposition can head off the IWC strategy of precarization of the labor market, and of pitting against each other those social segments which find themselves confronting the same market. On a small or a large scale, the potentials for molecular revolution appear every time that processes of detotalization and of deterritorialization encroach on the stratification of corporatism. Now, if it's true that the fundamental question is the inversion of the corporatist tendency, it seems equally true that the motor of that diminution of "social entropy" resides in consistently making a decompartmentalization of productive society the revolutionary project. And not only as an ideal horizon, as a communist ethics, but above all as a strategic struggle capable of taking the movement out of its current "failure neurosis." The most demoralizing situations and the most negative comparisons of apparent strength can rapidly change as soon as the precariousness of the current forms of IWC domination appears in an even more pronounced way. Even the most "conservative" segments of the working class are beginning to manifest their unrest, their impatience, and their disgust in regard to those who are supposed to represent them. The idea, for so long accepted in good faith, by virtue of which there existed only one political economy as a reference point – that of IWC – has had its day. The dismantling of companies, of branches of industries, of entire regions, the social and ecological costs of the crisis can no longer be written off as a necessary reconversion of the system. In fact, it has been clear for some time that this is not an ordinary crisis, but a radical attempt to destroy more than half a century's worth of "acquired advantages" and social victories of the reformism which corresponded to the previous forms of capitalism.

Obviously this does not mean that capitalism is in the process of collapsing on its own and that we have come, almost despite ourselves, to the eve of the "Great Night." What is certain is that capitalism and/or socialism intend to install a regime of frenzied disciplinarization over the entire planet, in which each segment of the collective labor force, each people, each ethnic group will be forced to submit to permanent control. In this regard, the guaranteed workers will be placed under the same regime as the precarious, and everything will be nuances, minute non-empirical transitions. No longer will anyone be able to assume a true statutory guarantee.

The traditional working classes should resign themselves to this. But what could the meaning of their revolt be if they do not understand that they no longer represent a social majority – neither numerically, nor as an ideal value, not even as a produced economic value? They are obliged, if they want to legitimate their rebellion, to socially recompose themselves, in alliance with the immense mass of exploited people, of marginalized people, which includes the large majority of young, women, immigrants, the sub-proletariats of the Third World and minorities of every kind. The principle task has become the reunification of the traditional components of the class struggle against exploitation with the new liberation movements and communist projects.

It is on this terrain that the new lines of alliance will be drawn. We draw a line through the tradition of the Third International, a black line over its totalitarian and/or corporatist results. A new revolutionary movement is in search of itself. It is born both inside and outside the traditional workers' movement; it proliferates and potentially converges along a front intrinsically unified by exploitation. It will destroy the repressive norms of the workday and of the capitalist appropriation of the totality of lifetime. New domains of struggle become possible everywhere. But the privileged point, the hot point in the production of new machines of revolutionary struggle resides within the zones of marginalized subjectivity. And there as well, it goes without saying, not in and of themselves – but because they are inscribed in the meaning of creative production processes considered in their evolutionary position, that is, not arbitrarily isolated within the capitalist economic sphere.

The social imaginary can recompose itself only through radical changes. In this regard, one should take into account that marginal phenomena are part of a context which does not define them as being at the margin, but which, on the contrary, confers on them a central place in the capitalist strategy. The marginal subjectivities, in as much as they are the product and the best "analysers" of command tendencies, are also those which resist it the best. The physical, bodily, plastic and external aspects of the liberation experiences of marginal subjects become equally the material of a new form of expression and creation. Language and image here are never ideological but always incarnated. Here, more than anywhere else, one can find the symptoms of the appearance of a new right to transformation and communitarian life, under the impetus of subjects in revolt.

New alliances: as a project of the production of singularities and as the possibility of conferring on this project a subversive social meaning. The self-analytical method of the forms of social subjectivity becomes revolutionary substance in the sense that it permits the semiotic understanding and political amplification of the implosion points of corporatism and the upheaval of its own lines of alliance. The common consciousness has already perceived this process of conjunction; the revolutionary imagination has begun to apprehend it; what remains is to make it the basis of the constitution of the future movement.

6. THINK AND LIVE IN ANOTHER WAY

PROPOSITIONS

Resentment, empty repetition and sectarianism are the modalities by which we live the betrayed hopes of the traditional workers' movement. For all that we do not renounce the history of struggles; on the contrary, we celebrate it because it is an integral part of our mental coordinates and sensibility. If we are dwarves on the shoulders of giants, we assume the benefits as much as the deplorable aspects of their heritage. At any rate, we want to move forward. Reuniting with the human roots of communism, we want to return to the sources of hope, that is, to a being-for, to a collective intentionality, turned toward doing rather than toward a being against, secured to impotent catchphrases of resentment. It is in real history that we intend to explore and experience the many realms of possibility which we call forth from everywhere. Let a thousand flowers bloom on the terrains which attempt to undermine capitalist destruction. Let a thousand machines of life, art, solidarity, and action sweep away the stupid and sclerotic arrogance of the old organizations! What does it matter if the movement trips over its own immaturity, over its spontaneism – its power of expression will ultimately only be reinforced. Without even being aware of it, despite the cacophony of the molecular movements which sustain it, an organizational crystallization is opening, oriented in the direction of new collective subjectivities. "Let a thousand flowers blossom, a thousand machines of struggle and of life," is not an organizational slogan and even less an enlightened prediction, but an analytic key to the new revolutionary subjectivity, a given on the basis of which can be grasped the social characteristics and dimensions of the singularities of productive labor. It is through an analysis of the real that they will be recomposed and will multiply as a subversive and innovative presence. The enemy has been incarnated in current forms of social command, through the elimination of differences and the imposition of a reductive logic of domination. Bringing to light the hegemony of singularization processes on the horizon of social production constitutes today the specific hallmark of communist political struggle.

The development, defense and expression of changing productive subjectivities, of dissident singularities, and of new proletarian temperments has become, in some respects, the primary content and task of the movement. That can take the form of the struggle on the welfare front, for the establishment of a guaranteed egalitarian income, against poverty in all its forms, for the defense and enlargement of alternative rights, and against the mechanisms of corporatist division... If one wants, one will find there as well the tradition of struggles against rent, and this such that it is not only fundamental, real, and financial, but that it is essentially undergirded by the articulations of capitalist command; i.e. a political rent, a rent reflecting position in the hierarchy of corporatist strata. New subjective components of production and revolution will find their first intervention opportunity at this level, redefining it in a positive mode as a liberation struggle against corporatist slavery and reactionary structures of production and as affirming the processes of singularity as an essential spring of social production.

This recomposition of the revolutionary movement implies, of course, immense efforts of courage, patience, and above all, intelligence. But what progress has already been made compared to preceding periods of struggle – which were indefatigable and often despairing – by the first groups conscious of this problematic, who only rarely succeeded in opening breaches in the union ghetto or in the political monopoly of the supposed labor parties! Here as well, life time must be imposed on production time. At this crossroads the second task of the revolutionary communist movement will be posed: consciously organizing the collective labor force independently of the capitalist and/or socialist structures, that is, of everything which touches on the production and reproduction of the mode of life. One thing, an effect, is to reveal new social productive forces and another is to organize them outside and against capitalist and/or socialist structures.

The development of science and technology and their massive incorporation in this transformation program are necessary, but not sufficient, conditions. No transformation is conceivable unless the entire field of productive labor is confronted with large movements of collective experimentation which break those conceptions which relate to profit centered capitalist accumulation.

It is in this direction that the expansion power of the collective labor force should be grasped. Thus a double movement will be established, like that of the human heart, between the diastole of the expansive force of social production and the systole of radical innovation and rearrangement of the workday. The movement of the social proletariat and new collective subjectivities must lay siege to the corporations, viz. the stakes regarding legislation governing the length of the workday, and impose its redefinitions and its permanent experimentation. They must impose not only a productive renewal, but also new ways of imagining and of studying production.

Think, live, experiment, and struggle in another way: such will be the motto of a working class which can no longer perceive itself as self-sufficient and which has everything to win by renouncing its arrogant myths of social centrality. As soon as one has finished with this sort of mystification, which ultimately has only profited the capitalist and/or socialist power formations, one will discover the great significance of the new lines of alliance which tie together the multiform and multivalent social stages at the heart of our era's productive forces. It is time that communism's imagination raise itself to the height of the changing waves which are in the process of submerging the old dominant realities.

Now it is necessary to introduce certain considerations regarding a first diagrammatic proposition integrating the definitions of the perspectives just introduced. It's only too evident that every effort at taking control of the length of the work day, by the movement of the new subjectivities, will be illusory if it does not attack frontally the network of command put in place by IWC. To tackle this network means putting in question the East-West relation, to derail the mechanism integrating the two superpowers, which has overcoded, from the 1970s until today, all international relations. Breaking the relation of domination laboriously established between capitalism and socialism, and radically reversing the alliances – especially the European ones – in the direction of the North-South axis, against the East-West axis, constitutes an essential foundation for recomposing the intellectual and working class proletariat in the advanced capitalist countries. A basis of social production which will win its independence against hierarchical oppression and the command of the great powers; a basis which only has meaning if it begins with a collective will to create alternative flows and structures to those of the East-West relation.

We are not fallbacks to "Third World-ism"; we do not pretend to transform it by way of a traditional "insurrectionism"; neither for all that do we believe in its independent capacity for development and "redemption" – at least in the current capitalist context. None of the successful revolutions in the developed countries has succeeded in transforming in a lasting way the structures of the state. It is not likely that those of the Third World will do any better. No, it is rather toward revolutionary cooperation and aggregation of forces among the intellectual and working proletariat of the North with the great mass of the proletariat of the South that it is necessary to turn to fulfill this historic task. All of this may seem Utopian, even extravagant, because today we, the workers and intellectuals of the countries of the North, are slaves of corporatist politics, of segmentary divisions, of the logic of profit, of blocking and extermination operations, of the fear of nuclear war, as they are imposed on us and with which we make ourselves accomplices. Our liberation requires creating a project and a practice which unifies, in the same revolutionary will, the intellectual forces and the proletariats of the North and of the South.

As the union of processes of singularity advances toward the project of reinventing communism, the problem of power will be posed with increasing acuity; it remains at the heart of the antagonism between proletarian components and the capitalist and/or socialist state. The traditional workers' movement wanted to respond to this question in a simple and radical way through the conquest of state power, then through the progressive disappearance of the State. Everything was supposed to follow from itself. One would oppose destruction with destruction and terror with terror. It would be useless today to provide an epilogue regarding the fictive and mystifying character of this dialectic or to underline the scandalous reference by holders of this doctrine to the heroic experience of the Paris Commune.

The first basic task of the revolutionary communist movement consists in having done with this sort of conception and in affirming the movement's radical separation not only from the state which it directly confronts but also, more fundamentally, from the very model of the capitalist state and all its successors, replacements, derived forms, and assorted functions in all the wheels of the socius, at all levels of subjectivity. Thus, to the struggles around welfare, against the organization of productive labor and of labor's social time, and to communitarian initiatives in this domain, should be added questioning the State as the determinant of different forms of oppression, the machine for overdetermining social relations, in order to reduce, block, and radically subjugate them, under the threat of its forces of death and destruction.

This question leads us to formulate a second diagrammatic proposition of communism and liberation: it concerns the urgency of reterritorializing political practice. Confronting the State today means fighting against this particular formation of the State, which is entirely integrated into IWC.

After Yalta, political relations were further emptied of their territorial legitimacy and drifted toward levels impossible to attain. Communism represents tendential destruction of those mechanisms which make of money and other abstract equivalents the only territories of man. This does not imply nostalgia for native lands, the dream of a return to primitive civilizations or to the supposed communism of the "good savage." It is not a question of denying the levels of abstraction which the deterritorialized processes of production made man conquer.

What is contested by communism are all types of conservative, degrading, oppressive reterritorialization imposed by the capitalist and/or socialist state, with its administrative functions, institutional organs, its collective means of normalization and blockage, its media, etc…. The reterritorialization induced by communist practice is of an entirely different nature; it does not pretend to return to a natural or universal origin; it is not a circular revolution; rather it allows an ungluing of the dominant realities and significations, by creating conditions which permit people to make their territory, to conquer their individual and collective destiny within the most deterritorialized flows.

(In this regard, one is led to distinguish very concretely: the movements of nationalist reterritorialization – Basque, Palestinian, Kurdish… which assume, to a certain extent, the great deterritorialized flows of Third World struggles and immigrant proletariats, and the movements of reactionary nationalist reterritorialization.)

Our problem is to reconquer the communitarian spaces of liberty, dialog and desire. A certain number of them are starting to proliferate in different countries of Europe. But it is necessary to construct, against the pseudo-reterritorializations of IWC (example: the decentralization of France, or of the Common Market), a great movement of reterritorializing bodies and minds: Europe must be reinvented as a reterritorialization of politics and as a foundation for reversing the alliances of the North-South axis. The third task of the revolutionary communist movement is thus also to disarticulate and dismantle the repressive functions of the State and its specialized apparatuses. This is the sole terrain on which new collective subjects confront the initiatives of the State, and only in the sense that the latter dispatches its teutonic cavaliers over those areas liberated by the revolutionary arrangements. Forces of love and humor should be put to work here so that they are not abolished, as is usually the case, in the mortally abstract and symbolic lunar image of their capitalist adversary! Repression is first and foremost the eradication and perversion of the singular. It's necessary to combat it within real life relations of force; it's also necessary to get rid of it in the registers of intelligence, imagination, and of collective sensitivity and happiness. Everywhere it's necessary to extract, including from oneself, the powers of implosion and despair which empty reality and history of their substance.

The state, for its part, can live out its days in the isolation and encirclement reserved for it by a reconstructed civil society! But if it appears about to come out of its retreat and to reconquer our spaces of freedom, then we will respond by submerging it within a new kind of general mobilization, of multiform subversive alliances. Until it dies smothered in its own fury.

The fourth task: Here we are inevitably returning to the anti-nuclear struggle and to the struggle for peace. Only, now it is in relation to a paradigm which brings to light the catastrophic implications of science's position in relation to the State, a position which presupposes a dissociation between the legitimacy of power and the goal of peace. It is truly a sinister mockery that states accumulate thousands of nuclear warheads in the name of their responsibility to guarantee peace and international order although it is evident that such an accumulation can only guarantee destruction and death. But this ultimate "ethical" legitimation of the state, to which reaction attaches itself as to a rampart, is also in the process of collapsing, and not only on a theoretical level, but also in the consciousness of those who know or suspect that collective production, freedom, and peace are in their proper place fundamentally irreducible to power.

Prevent the catastrophe of which the state is the bearer while revealing the extent to which that catastrophe is essential to the state. It remains true that "capitalism carries war as clouds carry storms." But, in a manner different than in the past, through other means and on a horizon of horror which at this point escapes all possible imagination, this perspective of the final holocaust has, in effect, become the basis of a veritable world civil war conducted by capitalist power and constituted by a thousand permanently erupting, pulverizing wars against social emancipation struggles and molecular revolutions. Nevertheless, in this domain, as in no other, nothing is fated. Not all the victories and defeats of the movement's new lines of alliance are inscribed in a mechanistic causality or a supposed dialectic of history. Everything is to be redone, everything is constantly to be reconsidered. And it's good that it is so. The state is only a cold monster, a vampire in interminable agony which derives vitality only from those who abandon themselves to its simulacra.

In 1968, no one could imagine that war would so quickly become such a close and encroaching horizon. Today, war is no longer a prospect: it has become the permanent frame of our lives.

The third great imperialist war has already begun. A war no doubt grows old after thirty years, like the Thirty Years War, and no one recognizes it any longer; even though it has become the daily bread of certain among the press. Yet such has resulted from capitalism's reorganization and its furious assaults against the world proletariats. The third diagrammatic proposition of communism and liberation consists in becoming aware of this situation and assuming the problematic of peace as fundamental to the process of reversing alliances along the North-South axis. Less than ever, peace is not an empty slogan; a formula of "good conscience"; a vague aspiration.

Peace is the alpha and omega of the revolutionary program. The anguish of war sticks to our skin, pollutes our days and nights. Many people take refuge in a neutralist politics. But even this unconsciousness generates anguish. Communism will tear men and women away from the stupidity programmed by IWC and make them face the reality of this violence and death, which the human species can conquer if it succeeds in conjugating its singular potentials of love and of reason.

And finally, to these alliances of productive organization and liberated collective subjectivities should be added a fifth dimension – of which we have already spoken amply – that of organization itself. The time has come to move from sparse resistance to constituting determinate fronts and machines of struggle which, in order to be effective, will lose nothing of their richness, their complexity, of the multivalent desires that they bear. It belongs to us to work for this transition.

To sum up: five tasks await the movements of the future: the concrete redefinition of the workforce; taking control over and liberating the time of the work day; a permanent struggle against the repressive functions of the state; constructing peace and organizing machines of struggle capable of assuming these tasks.

These five tasks are made diagrammatic by three propositions: contribute to reorienting the lines of proletarian alliance along a North-South axis; conquer and invent new territories of desire and of political action, radically separated from the State and from IWC; fight against war and work at constructing the proletariat's revolutionary movement for peace.

We are still far from emerging from the storm; everything suggests that the end of the leaden years will still be marked by difficult tests; but it is with lucidity, and without any messianism, that we envisage the reconstruction of a movement of revolution and liberation, more effective, more intelligent, more human, more happy than it has ever been.

Rome, Rebibbia Prison / Paris
1983-84

POSTSCRIPT, 1990
ANTONIO NEGRI

"Rome, Rebibbia Prison/Paris, 1983-1984": this chronological note which concludes our French text, published in 1985, has nothing contrived about it. The dialogue between the two authors did not come to a halt during the long years in which one of them was imprisoned. In fact in the last year of that imprisonment we had decided to collaborate on a work that would deal with the continuity of the communist political program, beyond the repression and in spite of its effects. When one of us left prison and went into exile, the possibility arose in 1984 to actually collaborate on such a project.

That is how this text was born. The continuity of the communist program, the memory of our struggles, and a political and ethical fidelity to the revolutionary option all contributed to renew our friendship and our discussions. It is scarcely necessary to recall how dreary that period was. In Italy, the so-called "years of lead" never seemed to end, and with them there had developed a leaden political and social climate; in France, the social democrats, having reached power with a program of profound social renewal, had by then transformed their politics and were carrying out the sinister business of restructuring which had been entrusted to them by capital; within the Atlantic alliance the reactionary adventures of Reagan and Thatcher had reached their apex; and in the USSR (as we only now can perceive) what were to be the very last – though still ferocious – remnants of Stalinism still held power.

Nothing seemed to threaten this horrible immobility – except for a bit of background noise, an occasional "limited" or "local" war, such as the "little" bloodbath between Iran and Iraq, the reemergence of collective cannibalism in Southeast Asia, and the fascism and apartheid of Latin America and South Africa. We were living in a period of permanent counterrevolution. The new movements that would become important in the second half of the 1980s – movements based on mobility and organization, anti-racist movements, movements rich in non-material desires – all of these had not yet appeared on the horizon. Instead those movements that had persisted through the 1970s lingered on, pathetic, enfeebled, and desperate.

Exactly against this background we decided to write once more of revolution, renewing a discourse of hope.

Ours was a discourse of hope, and a breaking away in a positive sense. But no one, not even friends, seemed to understand – our position was strange, improvised, out of fashion. We were not concerned with these objections, however, because we were interested in only one thing: reconstituting a nucleus, however small, of militancy and of subjectivity-in-progress. This meant resisting the political defeat of the 1970s, especially where it had been followed, on the capitalist side, with the production of an ideology of repentance, betrayal and self-pity, seasoned with the new, "weak" values of ethical cynicism, political relativism, and monetary realism.

Playing the card of naiveté, we wanted to affirm that it was still possible to live and to produce revolutionary subjectivity.

If this was our basic message, it was nevertheless not irrelevant how we went about expressing and objectifying our desire. Rereading ourselves today we can recognize that the themes of the analysis and the program of action proposed were and still remain essentially sound. In other words, the way we described the lines of development of the mode of production, the system of domination, and the crisis in both – and, on the other side, the prospects we outlined for the development of an alternative organization, as well as our judgments on the processes of constituting a new subject, on that subject's productive qualities, and on the cultural system that would constitute the subject – all of these elements of our analysis had been articulated in a way that captured the real trends. If we had made mistakes, they were errors of incompleteness – we hadn't risked pursuing the tendencies far enough, and we hadn't risked making our imagination revolutionary enough.

In brief: while the greater part of our analysis has been confirmed by subsequent events, certain elements have been contradicted, not by the historical developments, but by the intensity – foreseen – which those developments assumed. Let us review some of these elements.

a. We recognized very clearly that work, as it became more and more abstract, mobile, and socially diffused, required new forms of recomposition. We began to follow the processes involved in producing the subjectivity which the new organization of capitalist production entailed. But we should have gone more deeply and realized that this newly produced subjectivity was locked in an insuperable contradiction, for social cooperation was more and more violently in opposition to the structures of capitalist control. The contradiction was especially apparent in the case of intellectual work, which is immaterial and which, as it became the center of production, manifested its irreconcilable difference with the capitalist norm. We ought to have noted more clearly the central importance of the struggles within the schools, throughout the educational system, in the meanders of social mobility, in the places where the labor force is formed; and we also ought to have developed a wider analysis of the processes of organization and revolt which were just beginning to surface in those areas.

b. There was certainly no mistaking the new dimension assumed by communications, which functioned as an instrument and promoter of deterritorialization, directed toward intellectual usurpation and moral impoverishment. And it was no paradox if exactly here, in this area where capitalist domination was so strong, one could detect mechanisms for recomposing the subject and giving a new territorialization to desire. But while our work stopped at the point of identifying the possibility of such a rebellion, we should have persisted in our analysis, tracing out the new moments of reconstruction, of recomposition of the subject. This latter process needs to be seen not in the context of some homemade operation, or some unique experiment. We are not talking about some Utopia to come, but about a real formative power, a material force for political and social reconstruction.

c. We should have better defined the scope of the ecological struggle, a movement which appeared consistent with the program of proletarian liberation. We ought to have acknowledged not only the necessity of defending nature against the menace of destruction and the imminent apocalypse that hangs over it, but also the urgency of constructing new systems and conditions for reproducing the human species, as well as defining the modes and timetables for revolutionary action in this direction. It is easy to see that our text was written before Chernobyl.

d. And now we must take up the point most deserving of criticism and self-censure. In defining Integrated World Capitalism, we did not sufficiently measure the intensity of the process set in motion by the direct participation of the Soviet Union in that mechanism. Of course all through our pamphlet we had insisted on the identity of the exploitation taking place in capitalist countries and that taking place in socialist countries. Now the world market's definitive overcoming of the Stalinist pressure only confirms this observation. But the acceleration of the processes of integration taking place in the last five years and the effects thereof cannot be underestimated. Very acute contradictions are being created within each of the two blocs as well as in the relationship between East and West. The problem of peace can be put in much less utopian terms today than when we composed our pamphlet. But precisely for that reason, the achievement and the maintenance of peace become a positive force for reopening the processes of liberation, revolt, and radical transformation.

e. Certainly our book did not underestimate the question of North-South relations. But we were far too optimistic. We believed that in the face of the disastrous decline in the prospects of the Southern nations, some kind of new alliance with the North would inevitably be laid out. Nothing of the sort occurred, and indeed the situation has become much worse. Entire continents are adrift without a compass and there has not been a single political initiative worthy of the name which has been offered to combat the enormous problems posed by this disaster. Benefit concerts and acts of state-sponsored charity have multiplied – and at the same time the isolation and the lack of news from these poorest countries have become more ominous.

It is with desperation and anguished impotence that we look upon that massacre of innocents, that unending genocide... It is with anger that we contemplate these things.

We could continue analyzing the defects of our discourse, while still affirming its substantial validity. But to what end? The evidence that allows us to still believe today that communism has never been nearer to fruition derives not from our own words but from the radical change of direction taken by history in the last four or five years. What we once believed in as a utopia now seems common sense. The age of the Reagan counterrevolution and the very gloomy period of neoliberal power now seem definitively superseded. We knew that they would not last long, and we never ceased laughing at their "new philosophers" and being nauseated by those who had "repented." Nevertheless, we are surprised to see how fragile such arrogance really was. The grand declarations about neoliberalism, about a new social contract, about a new Enlightenment are today obviously charades – as they were in the past. In. the past, however, it took courage to say so; nowadays this truth seems banal.

But we are not so much interested in talking as in being. Being, and thus organizing. Organizing, and hence having the possibility of overthrowing the sense of production which capital, for the sake of profit, enforces within our information oriented social fabric. Overthrowing that sense, subverting it... For that we look to praxis. And praxis, today, is found in the East bloc.

Before speaking of praxis, a brief clarification of terminology is in order. People say that communism is dead. We think this affirmation is inexact, and that it is socialism which is moribund. How are these two terms distinguished? For the old-line militant, the distinction between socialism and communism was obvious: socialism was that political-economic order in which "to each was given according to his work "whereas communism was that system in which "to each was given according to his needs." Socialism and communism represented two different stages of the revolutionary process, the first being characterized by the socialization of the means of production and by the political administration of this transition, the second characterized by the extinction of the state and by the spontaneous management of both the economy and power.

If this distinction was clear to the old line communist militants, today, in the era of a collapse of "real socialism," it has been obliterated, and communism and socialism are easily confused. They are confused via a hostile, wholesale reduction performed by the adversaries of socialism, who have undertaken a brutal liquidation of all things socialist that were created in the world after 1917, whether in Eastern Europe or in the Third World. Of course these all too easy liquidations take sustenance from favorable conditions: in the socialist states of Eastern Europe during the last forty years the sole methods of legitimizing power have been the mystification of ideology, frauds perpetrated by the bureaucracy, and cynicism in dealing with theory – all of which, predictably enough, have produced symptoms of radical refusal and disgust. How could the "radiant future" promised by communism have avoided being discredited in societies that were socialist in name only, societies that were in fact bureaucratic organizations, in which utopia was achieved by hiding realities?

Having said this, let us return to the concepts themselves and their history, noting that, in all probability, they are not reducible to the guises in which they appear in present day polemics, nor subject to the current wholesale dismissals. Indeed for about a century and a half, that is, from the foundation of the "League of Communists" which looked to Marx for leadership in the middle of the last century, communism has been the central political ideology for the modern age. In opposition to the old utopias, it is based on a real, forward-looking analysis of the mechanism of development of capitalism from the worker's point of view. Taking a scientific look at the social-economic dynamics of the capitalist system as it lives and grows solely by exploiting the labor force, the party of the working class can define the strategies and tactics for the communist future, setting as its objectives the destruction of the mechanism of capitalist accumulation and the conquest of political power. Marx brings us up to this point, offering a formidable scientific apparatus for dealing with this project.

The subsequent transfer of Marx's theoretical analysis to the problem of revolutionary mobilization within the new context of European capitalism at the beginning of a century marked by a radical instability in the various political and social systems, is the task which Lenin takes up and which leads him to formulate the organizational principles of a new kind of party, the Bolshevik Communist Party. This party is the vanguard of the working class which, having broken with the mere economic demands of the unions, the mere opportunistic spontaneity of the anarchists, and the legalistic version of the class struggle practiced by the parties of the Second International, has shaped itself into a disciplined, flexible instrument specifically adapted for seizing power and installing the dictatorship of the proletariat. The objective of this dictatorship is the institution of socialism, or the nationalization of the means of production and a centralization of planning. But all of this was supposed to take place within a radical process of democratic participation, within a transitional period that would create conditions of economic growth for everyone and at the same time would dissolve the central power of the state and the law, bestowing both wealth and freedom on the citizens. What an illusion, and what disappointments!

The Leninist conceptions of the party and the revolutionary transition were contested within the left wing of the workers' movement by Rosa Luxemburg, both at the time of the 1905 uprising and after the 1917 revolution. For her, organization meant the permanent refusal, exactly in the workplace, of any mediation of workers' self-expression or the class struggle through the agency of the unions or the reformist party; her idea of organization coincided with the rising levels of worker spontaneity and with the specific political institutions generated by such spontaneity, including the soviets in Russia in 1905 and 1917, and the workers' councils in Germany in 1918-1919. Lenin, on the other hand, held that the workers' own self-directed organization for struggle could not prefigure the party, since a revolutionary political directorate, standing outside the individual struggles, would have to supervise all the various expressions of spontaneity in order to assure the fundamental goal of a dictatorship of the proletariat.

Is it this contradiction between Luxemburg and Lenin – between an idea of communism as a democracy constituted by masses in struggle, or, on the other hand, as a dictatorship of the proletariat – that gives rise to the crisis in the management of socialist power once the insurrection has been victorious and power has been seized? Many communists (and there are still many of them in the world) think so, and it is very probable that as the subversive movement revives in the coming decades (for it is evident that it will revive) It will have to reconsider these issues.

But other problems can also become central in the discussions motivated by the present crisis of communism and the collapse of "real socialism." In particular, it is interesting to follow developments in Russia in the wake of the dilemma that surfaced after Lenin's death. At that point the Soviet political debate centered on the two alternatives of a "permanent revolution," or, on the other hand, "socialism in a single country." These alternatives were discussed in terms of their relationship to Leninism and to the October revolution. Leon Trotsky, an ardent defender of the first thesis as a means of inoculating the revolution against the bureaucratization of the state and the party, was defeated by those who, embracing the second alternative, believed that the unequal development of capitalist countries and the exceptional nature of a proletarian victory at the weak link in the imperialist chain had rendered the construction of socialism in a single country an obligatory course of action. Among the advocates of the second thesis Stalin soon emerged as the merciless executor of an extreme centralization of the party and an enormous concentration of power in the administrative-repressive apparatus. Thus the distance between Marx's theory of a class struggle against the capitalist system and the actual practice in the construction of socialism widened vertiginously. Paradoxically, communism – defined by Marx as "the real movement which abolishes the present state of affairs" – became the productive activity which created at whatever cost the material bases of an industrial society that was locked in a competition with the rhythm of its own development and with that of the capitalist countries.

Socialism did not commit itself to overcoming the capitalist system and the system of wage labor, but instead became a social-economic alternative of capitalism.

Can we thus claim that the present crisis of "real socialism" amounts to nothing more than the crisis in the socialist management of capital? That the present situation has nothing to do with any ultimate crisis of communism? We can indeed make such claims if, having accepted the lessons of a century and a half of history, we reassert with the greatest possible emphasis the distinction between socialism and communism. For the first is nothing more than one of the forms in which capital can be organized and administered – and that is why most of the advanced capitalist countries today have economic systems in which the socialist component is extremely strong. But communism is the form in which society can be organized after the destruction of both the capitalist system, that is, after the destruction of the class system and the system of exploitation, when the organizing role of the state, as opposed to that of society, has been cancelled. We must further insist that it is absolutely untrue that socialism is a phase of, or an instrument of transition toward, communism. Historically speaking, the exact contrary has been true, for the most ferocious forms of political and economic oppression have occurred within "real socialism," whose so-called "new socialist man" was nothing other than a perfected form of the beast of burden. As Marx teaches us, communism is born directly from class antagonism, from the refusal of both work and the organization of work, whether in the bourgeois form or the socialist form. The new modes of this antagonism and this refusal can be seen in Western Europe, but are even more apparent today in the East bloc's crisis of "real socialism." That is why the revolt in the eastern European nations constitutes a strong incentive for a renewed discussion and a renewed militancy within communism. The need to distinguish between "socialism" and "communism" has once again become obvious: but this time not because of the blurred boundaries between them, but because they are so opposed. Socialism is nothing other than one of the forms taken by capitalist management of the economy and of power, whereas communism is an absolutely radical political economic democracy and an aspiration to freedom.

What do the events in Eastern Europe reveal to us? First of all – and we have already recognized this – they mark the end of the illusion that there might be shortcuts to communism. Whatever might have been the beliefs of our predecessors, whether workers by profession or intellectuals in the vanguard, we must acknowledge that there can be no progress, no transition from capitalism to communism via socialism. Communism, thus, is the minimum essential program. It can and must be constructed starting from the conditions of socialist and/or capitalist society – within these conditions. There are not two or three or four or n phases or stages of development: there is only one, and that is the retaking of freedom into one's own hands and the construction of collective means for controlling cooperation in production. This single stage of development allows us to discover to what extent capitalism and/or socialism have rendered production social, abstract and shared, and it also permits us to reorganize this cooperation outside and against the capitalist system of command, outside and against the daily theft of power and wealth which is perpetrated by the few at the expense of the whole society.

Communism is already alive within the capitalist and/or socialist societies of today, in the form of a secret order dedicated to cooperation in production: an order covered up by the capitalist system of command and/or bureaucracy, crushed between the opposing forces of those who command and those who follow commands, a new order which strains to become manifest but cannot. In the East bloc we saw mass protest explode in the form of a pure negation of the past.

But we also saw the expression of a potential that was unknown to us in the West: in the Eastern European nations we saw a fully alive civil society come to the surface, one that had not been homogenized, one capable of expressing a collective political will in a way no longer found in the West – a drive for power founded on the social base rather than on the forms of the state. I am certain that in the West as well all of this will take place, and quite soon – for what has happened in the East was not born from the special experience of those countries.

What took place in the East is the beginning of a revolt against a capitalism which had reached the apex of its tyranny. There are always those imbeciles who identify capitalist development with the number of computers sold: of course in that case one would have to believe that there was no capitalism in the East and that its revolution will quickly be calmed by selling computers. And there are those who will attempt this strategy. But that is not really how things stand: the level of capitalist development is defined by the degree of social cooperation in production. From this point of view, the Eastern bloc is in no way behind the West.

It is against this background that we read the revolution which has exploded; and we further suggest that, as with all revolutions that are truly such, this one will spread – from the East to the West, a new 1968, moving in the opposite direction.

What else do the events in the East reveal? Another element, less visible to the majority of the public, but nonetheless extraordinarily important: the birth of a new model of democracy. In our civilization we are accustomed to thinking that there is only one model of democracy, the Western one, and that it need only be applied generally.

History has come to an end, there is nothing more to invent, and Western democracy and the "American way of life" represent the absolutely final product of the human spirit! All of this is an arrogant illusion. What has happened in the East demonstrates just the opposite, for (despite what Hegel says) not only has the world spirit not finished its travels, but in fact it gives signs of having reversed its course, returning from across the Atlantic and heading east, toward the Russian steppes. That is where it has been reborn, and that is where the debate about democracy is taking place. Democracy cannot be simply political emancipation, but must include social and economic liberation. No democracy is possible unless the problems of work and of command are solved. Every form of democratic government must also be a form of liberation from the slavery of work, must yield a new, free organization of cooperation in production. It is not a question of putting factories and the organization of social work in the hands of new bosses, entrusting them to the hypocritical freedom of the marketplace, handing them back to the exploitative desires of capitalists and bureaucrats. Rather, it is a question of understanding what might be the rules for the democratic management of economic entrepreneurship. An impossible utopia? Fewer and fewer people think so. Not only in the East but even in the West, more and more people are asking themselves how to achieve a democracy that includes the democratic management of production. And their stupefaction is directed not at communism, but at the present form of production — their amazement (and their grief) derive from the fact that every day we are compelled to witness the persistence of figures as obsolete and useless as the capitalist and bureaucratic bosses. In the East, within the revolution, people are experiencing a new form of democracy: the democracy of work, a communist democracy.

A third lesson has reached us from the East bloc. Who has revolted? The working class? In part yes, but often not. The middle classes, then? To a fair degree, but only when they were not linked to the bureaucracy. What about the students, scientists, workers linked to advanced technologies, intellectuals, and in short, all those who deal with abstract and intellectual work? Certainly this represents the nucleus of the rebellion. Those who rebelled, in brief, were the new kind of producers. A social producer, manager of his own means of production and capable of supplying both work and intellectual planning, both innovative activity and a cooperative socialization. From this point of view as well, what has happened in the East is not foreign to us: indeed we might say, "de te fabula narratur." For in the countries where capitalism reigns idiotic and triumphant, corrupt and incapable of self-criticism, arrogant and confused, here as well the subject who constantly proposes to revolt is the same: the new productive subject, intellectual and abstract, students, scientists, workers linked to advanced technologies, university workers, etc. It is because of this subject with whom we identify that the events of the East pertain to us. Whether Gorbachev remains in power or is removed by Ligachev, whether perestroika succeeds in the present form or in a second wave that will inevitably follow, whether the Russian empire endures or not — these are all problems that concern only the Soviets.

We have our Cossacks to defeat, and there are many of them, and we are very late in joining the battle. Nonetheless we are grateful to the Soviets for having initiated, for the second time in this century, a profound process in the renewal of the spirit. It is a process that we believe to be irreversible, not only in Russia, but also in the life of humankind.

Antonio Negri, Paris Christmas 1989

APPPENDIX ONE
THE NEW SPACES OF FREEDOM
FÉLIX GUATTARI

We might refuse to resign ourselves to it, but we know for a fact that both in the East and in the majority of the Third World rights and liberties are subject to the discretionary powers of the political forces in charge of the state. Yet we are not so ready to admit, and often refuse to confront, the fact that they are equally threatened in the West, in countries that like to call themselves 'champions of the free world'.

This hard question, so close to the skin and pregnant with dramatic human implications, is hardly resolved if we remain at a level of statements of principle. It would be impossible to fail to recognize the fact that for a dozen years a whole bundle of rights and freedoms and a whole series of spaces of freedom continued to lose ground in Europe. If we consider what is happening to immigrants and the distortions that the right to political asylum is undergoing in France alone this fact is manifestly unequivocal. But the defeat stares us in the face even when detached from mere narrow jurisprudence, when considering the actual evolution of the 'right' to dispose of basic material means of survival and labor for millions of people in Europe (the unemployed, young and old people, the precarious); the 'right to difference' for all kinds of minorities; and the 'right' to effective democratic expression for the large majority of peoples. Militants might object that the conflicts related to formal juridical freedoms should not be treated on par with the conquest of new spaces of freedom because only the latter is relevant to concrete struggles (to be fair, this reaction is reminiscing of an era that has long gone). Justice never kept out of the social fray (it never stood over and above social struggles); democracy was always more or less manipulated; there is nothing, no greatness, to be expected from the realm of formal juridical freedom, whilst, on the contrary, everything is still to be done when it comes to new spaces of freedom. As far as I'm concerned, after taking an interest in the extradition cases and political trials of Bifo, Klauss Croissant, Piperno, Pace, Francois Pain, Toni Negri and others, I was forced to revise my opinion on the importance of these supposedly formal freedoms. Today they seem to me almost completely inseparable from other freedoms 'on the ground', to speak like the ethnologists. Now more than ever we must refuse to remain at the level of a global denunciation of bourgeois justice: doing so would be formal indeed. The independence of the judiciary is often really nothing but a decoy; instead of resigning to this and returning to a mythology of spontaneity and the so-called 'people's tribunals', we should think of ways to make it actual. The specialization of social functions and the division of labor are what they are; besides, nothing would seem to justify any expectations of deep changes in public opinion in the short or medium term; and there is no way of hoping that organized societies will manage to do without a judicial apparatus any time soon! This does not mean that we have to accept it as it is, quite the opposite: it is crucial to redefine its mode of development, its competences, its means, and its possible articulations in a democratic environment... To do so struggles for freedoms must also be given new instruments to take us forward:

- Ad hoc interventions in practical affaires where rights and freedoms are undermined;
- Longer term activities, such as liaising with groups of lawyers, magistrates, social workers and prisoners

... in view of developing alternative forms of systems of justice.

The struggles that defend the respect of the law and the offensive struggles aimed at conquering new realms of freedom are complementary. Both are set to become at least as important as trade union and political struggles, and to influence them more and more. This is the process that is apparently unfolding in France, with the growing role played by organizations such as Amnesty International, the League of Human Rights, France Terre d'Asile, the Cimade.

Despite the above premises we still cannot treat the evolution of freedoms in Europe as something in itself separate from the context of international tensions and world economic crises. But as soon as I mention these two things a new question starts humming in my ears. Should we regard these tensions and crises as *causes* of the weakening of freedoms, or, inversely, as the *outcome* of the rise of conservativism and reactionarism that followed the 1960s wave of struggles for freedoms? What I'd like to demonstrate is that our analysis of the tension between East and West and the world crisis would gain considerable grounds if we reconsidered them from the perspective of this question on freedoms.

I sometimes wonder whether in our societies, imprudently known as 'post-industrial', these freedoms are not destined to be irreversibly eroded by some kind of global rise in the entropy of social control. But this morose sociologism earns me nothing but days of depression! On dispassionate reflection, I see no reason to blame this repression on the proliferation of the mechanisms of information and communication in the machineries of production and social life. No! What distorts everything is something else! It is not techno-scientific 'progress', but the inertia of outmoded social relations: international relations between blocs and this permanent arms race that sucks the blood out of the economy and anaesthetizes its spirits! So I would be inclined to say that the international tension is probably less the result of a fundamental antagonism between two superpowers – as we are led to believe – than a means for them to actually 'discipline' the planet. In short, two chief gendarmes hold complementary roles, but not as in a puppet show, because here the blows really hurt! So the overall tension of the system grows and the hierarchical elements of its military, economic, social and cultural wings become exacerbated. Up there, in the Olympus of the Gods of War, much noise and many threats are made – as well as, unfortunately, many very dangerous things too! – so that at the bottom, at all levels, the flunkies are kept silent!

In this respect, the defense of individual and collective freedoms never was a serious issue in the conflict-ridden relations between the East and the West, and this is indicative. With proclamations and the parading of great principles put aside, it becomes apparent how little this issue weights on the important international 'deals' (President Carter managed to ridicule himself before the American political class by insisting more than was customary on this subject!). Western leaders would easily accommodate themselves to the techniques of the totalitarian bureaucracy of the Eastern block. And, under surface appearances and behind the ideological and strategic hype they seem to be carrying out similar policies and share the same set of objectives: namely to control individuals and social groups more and more closely and to normalize and integrate them, if possible facing no resistance from them and without them even realizing it – making use of Collective Infrastructures for their formation and 'maintenance', of the media to model their thinking and imaginary, and (no doubt in the future) of some sort of permanent computer radio control to allocate a territorial residence and economic trajectory to each on of them. The outcome is there, we can already see it! That is: a growing segregation that generates ethnic, sexual and age discrimination, greater freedom of action for the cast of bosses and managers, and more subservience from the pawns at the foundations of the big capitalist game. The decline of freedoms affecting more or less the whole world is mainly due to the growth of more conservative and functionalist conceptions of the world. These are reactionary but always ready to seize the 'progress' of science and technique, to put it at their service. We need to realize that this repression was only made possible by the political conjunction of the western bourgeoisie, 'socialist' bureaucracies and the corrupt 'elites' of the Third World, which together form a new figure of capitalism that I elsewhere defined as 'Integrated World Capitalism'.

The crisis and freedoms ... Of course they are related! Economic anxiety in itself weighs heavily on the spirits; it inhibits all desire for contestation and can even encourage paradoxical results, such as the shift of a fraction of the communist electorate towards Le Pen's National Front in France. But, even so, isn't the presentation of this problem in the mainstream mass media largely distorted? Is this crisis weighing on our freedoms or, rather, is it collective passivity, demoralization, disorientation and the lack of organization of potentially innovative forces to leave the field open for a new 'wild capitalism' to convert profit into socially devastating effects? On the one hand, the term 'crisis' is particularly ill-suited to denote the nature of the series of catastrophes that has been shaking the world, and primarily the Third World, for the past ten years. On the other hand, it would be completely illegitimate to circumscribe these phenomena to the economic sphere alone. Hundreds of millions of human beings are starving to death, billions of individuals are sinking into misery and despair year after year, and this is presented and explained to us as an economic problem that cannot be forecasted until the end of the crisis! Nothing can be done about it! This crisis falls from the sky; it comes and goes, like the hail of the Hurricane Hortense! Only the omens – these famous and distinguished economists – could possibly have something to say about it. But if there is a place where absurdity turns into infamy, this is it! Because in the end, what need would there be to associate industrial and economic restructuring – applied on a world scale and engaged in the deepest reorganization of the means of production and society – with such a mess? We need a 180 degree turn in the way we think through these problems, and urgently. The political takes precedence over the economic, not the other way around! Even though under present circumstances it would be difficult to assert that the political manufactures the crisis from scratch – in so far as it produces similar effects and catastrophic interactions that people no longer control, for example, between economic devastations and environmental disasters, or, in another realm, between the monetary system and the oil market – there isn't much more to be held responsible for the most pernicious social effects. And the end of the crisis, or, if you prefer, of this series of disasters, will either be political and social or it won't happen at all, and humanity will continue to make her way towards who knows what last implosion! Where does Europe stand in all this? Europe is often held up as a land of freedom and culture, so its vocation ought to be to stabilize the relations between the East and the West and initiate the promotion of a new international order between the North and the South. Whilst it is true that its German side recently started revealing all its interests in calming things down, we are still very far from an autonomous and coherent European policy. All the more so as France retreats into its traditional role of the Don Quixote of the protection of Western progress! In fact, Europe's freedom to act reduces, like shagreen, as it becomes more apparent that Europe is not going to emerge unscathed from this huge attempt at restructuration of world capitalism. Europe's feet and hands remain tied to the economic and monetary axiomatic strategy of the USA. More than ever, Europe is entangled in what the technocrats claim to be nationalist and statist 'archaisms' and all sorts of 'corporatism'. In order to develop a unitary movement within the people whom it is meant to unite, the European Economic Community has unearthed and deepened the very hatreds we thought had died out for a long time, and to make matters worse the whole of its Mediterranean flank slowly shifts towards an intermediary kind of Third World status.

Freedom is a right, above all! But not a vested right, at least. Concrete freedoms keep fluctuating along the path of power relations according to whether they are renounced or reaffirmed. In this respect, to avoid generalities and abstractions, it would be better to talk about *degrees of freedom*, or, rather, about *differential coefficients of freedom*. Human freedom has never existed all in one piece. Even in the borderline case of the solitude of ivory towers, freedom is only established in relation to others – starting from the blocks of identity interjected in the self. In practice, freedoms only unravel in relation to the rights established with close friends and neighbors, in relation to the subordination of those who are in my power, to the effects of intimidation and influence of the authorities that dominate me and, finally, in relation to the rules, codes and laws of different public domains. Just as the status of free citizen was established on the background of generalized slavery in ancient times, so do the freedoms of European white adults with a minimum income at their disposal find their 'standing' on the ground of the enslavement of the Third World today, both internally and externally. That is to say, in France, for instance, the most elementary wish to defend the rights of immigrants or protect the right to political asylum, even if devoid of outdated political theories or emanating from simple charity, could end up taking us very far because it puts under question not only the respect of formal rights but a whole conception of the world, of crucial axioms of segregation, racism, withdrawal, ideology of security, and the perspective of a Europe of police rather than a Europe of freedoms...

Respect of human rights in the East as in the West, in the North as in the South; peace and disarmament imposed on states through new waves of 'pacifist demoralization' ; the establishment, amongst the wealthy Third World countries, of relations that share the goal of contributing to the development of human potential: these could be the main international axes of a new social practice for the emancipation and conquest of spaces of freedoms. But these issues cannot feed into a body of meaningful struggles unless those who wish to act on them in practice appreciate the double nature of the obstacles that Integrated World Capitalism opposes to their project, namely:

> 1) an objective adversity that is constantly evolving due to the accelerated transformations of means of production and social relations;
> 2) a subjective stupefaction and a veritable industrial production of individual and collective subjectivity, that ensures the most formidable efficiency and obedience.

Before going any further I now wish to recall the conditions that future militant actions and machines of struggle for peace and freedom in all their forms need to be ready for. In my opinion – and I do not claim to have an exhaustive definition and a proposal that is 'ready to go' – we need to draw some lessons from the auspicious period of the 1960s and the defeat that followed it. We were naïve, disorganized, indiscriminate and well-informed, sometimes sectarian and narrow-minded, but often visionaries and oriented towards the future; obviously a future that would not resemble the image of our dreams! But I am convinced that we are faced again with a set of problems of method reminiscent of the ones of the struggles and organization of those times, and some lessons can be drawn from experience, the experiences to which some people sacrificed their best years. I see these conditions as follows:

> 1) New social practices of liberation will not establish hierarchical relations between themselves; their development will answer to a principle of *transversality* that will enable them to be established by 'traversing', as a 'rhizome', heterogeneous social groups and interests. The pitfalls to avoid are these:

a – The reconstitution of 'vanguard' and major state parties that dictate their law and mould their collective desires in a way that parallels – though formally antagonizes – that of a dominant system. The inefficiency and pernicious character of this kind of dispositif is no longer in need of demonstration;
b – The compartmentalization of militant practices and the singling out and separation between practices with political objectives of different scope, from the defense of sectarian interests to the transformation of everyday life ... and the separation between, on the one hand, programmatic and theoretical reflection and, on the other hand, an analytics of subjectivity of groups and individuals concretely engaged in action, which is to be invented from scratch.

This character of transversality of new social practices – the refusal of authoritarian disciplines, formal hierarchies, orders of priorities decreed from above, and compulsory ideological references – should not be seen in contradiction with the obviously inevitable, necessary and desirable establishment of *centers of decision* that use the most sophisticated technologies of communication and aim to maximum efficaciousness if necessary. The whole question here is to promote analytical collective procedures that allow for the dissociation of the *work of decision* from the *imaginary investments of power*; these only coincide in capitalist subjectivity because the latter lost its dimensions of singularity and converted into what might be called an Eros of equivalence (little does it matter the nature of my power, since I dispose of a certain capital of abstract power).

2) One of the main goals of new social practices of liberation will be the development of more than a simple protection: collective and/or individual *process-*

es of singularization. These are meant to include everything that confers to these initiatives a character of living subjectivation and irreplaceable experience, that 'is worth being lived', that 'gives meaning to life'... After iron decades of Stalinism, numerous returns to power of the social democrats – with the self same scenario of compromise, spinelessness, impotence and defeat – and the narrow minded and dishonest Boy Scout attitude of small groups, militancy ended up being impregnated with a rancid smell of church that has come to arouse a legitimate movement of rejection. Only its reinvention of new themes that start from a dissident subjectivity carried out by groups-subjects will make it possible to conquer again the abandoned terrains currently left to the prefabricated subjectivities of the media and Infrastructures of this new-look capitalism. And here we reiterate the need to invent a collective analytics of different forms of 'engaged' subjectivities. In this respect, we do not start completely from scratch. We have much to learn from the way the Greens in Germany or Solidarnosc in Poland have successfully managed to build new forms of militant life. We also have negative and inverse examples, such as the sectarianism of the Basque military ETA or the monstrous terrorist and dogmatic deviations of the Red Brigades in Italy that have inexorably led to the decapitation of the movement of liberation that had indisputably been the richest and most promising in Europe.

I repeat: the only means to avoid this deadly calamity is to provide the means of an analytical management of the processes of singularization or the 'making dissidence' of subjectivity.

3) These mutating militant machines for transversal and singularized spaces of freedom will not have any claim to durability. This way, they will come to terms with their intrinsic precariousness and the need for their continuous renewal, supported by a long lasting social movement of great scope.

This will lead them to forge *new and large alliances* that will make them avoid their most serious infantile disease: a tenacious propensity to experiencing oneself as a minority under siege. Here it is a case of promoting a logic of multivalent alliances, that avoid both the duplicitous combinations of power and the purist and sectarian dynamics of the movements of the 1960s that led to its definitive separation from the population en large. They will need to be sufficiently transversal and open to be able to communicate with social groups whose preoccupations, styles and points of view are very remote from theirs. This will only be possible in so far as they will take responsibility for their finitude and their singularity, and they will free themselves from the perverse myth of the *seizing of state power* by a vanguard party, without appeal or reservations.

Nobody will seize power in the name of the oppressed! Nobody will confiscate freedoms in the name of freedom. The only acceptable objective now is the seizing of society by society itself. The state! That is another problem. One should not oppose it in a frontal way, nor flirt with its degeneration to smoothen the way of tomorrow's socialism! In a sense, we have the state we deserve! By this I mean that the state is what remains as the most abject form of power when society has offloaded its collective responsibility. And time will not win over this monstrous secretion by itself; it is primarily organized practices that will enable society to disengage from the collective infantilism to which the media and capitalist infrastructures have condemned it. The state is no exterior monster that one needs to either flee or subdue. It is, starting from ourselves, at the root of our unconscious. We must 'do with' it. It is an incontrovertible fact of our life and of our struggle.

Transversality, singularization, and new alliances; here are the three ingredients that I would like to see poured profusely into the pot of freedoms. Then we can see the famous 'immaturity' of Europe and its well known 'archaisms' change their color. I dream of the day the Basques, the clandestines of Ulster, the Greens of Germany, Scottish and Welsh miners, immigrants, Polish pseudo-Catholics, Southern Italians and the nameless packs of dogs who refuse to understand or know anything that is offered to them will start screaming together: 'Yes, we are all archaic and you can put your modernity where you want!' So the passivity and demoralization will turn into a will to freedom and freedom into a material force that is able to change the course of a nasty history.

Montréal, November 1984

… APPPENDIX TWO
ARCHEOLOGICAL LETTER. OCTOBER 1984
ANTONIO NEGRI

I was invited to take part in a talk in Montreal and I am quite happy to do so, but I don't like the idea of just sending a contribution by mail. It would be perceived as a dry and arrogant gesture. So on second thought I decided that the best thing to do would be to ask you to read this letter at the convention – the last of the series of letters I've sent you, which deals, as usual, with our work on social practice. This way, you will have to intervene to clarify the assumptions underlying our discussion and maybe enter polemics with others and myself. So my rather dry contribution from afar can become warmer and closer, as is my desire to reengage in a productive discussion with our comrades after so many years of forced absence. Now it is obvious that, having traced some very general elements of the program in *New Lines of Alliance*, you and I had to turn to the question of social practice. The program will no doubt take on other forms; there is no need to formulate them. But it is also true that so much discredit and skepticism have befallen the topic of social practice in these last few years, so many denials, that we not only need to ask whether a social practice, i.e. a subversive and transformative militancy, is possible, but indeed if it is even possible to formulate a program and a communicable revolutionary discourse. To understand and eventually dispel these doubts, let's take a closer look at things.

For a long time, we were sure that the two possibilities, of program and of practice, were linked by a single proof. Whilst practice has to verify the truth of the program, the program only takes shape in so far as subjects put it into action. When I was younger, this was called "research in common"; we kept this virtuous and concrete circle alive within the class war. In the sixties, in the large factories of FIAT and petrochemicals, we only had one way of verifying the immediate practice and truth of the refusal to work, and that was bringing workplaces and factories to a halt. Our arrogant skepticism towards ideology was repaid for in practice by a very staunch criterion of truth. The mark of truth was its evidence. How Wittgensteinian our workers were! On this issue, today it would be easy, but probably unrealistic, to repeat the somewhat brutal motto *"Verum ipsum factum"* [it's true because it is]. Indeed, the problem of social practice doesn't seem to be solvable by repeating this kind of solution: neither by the theoretical repetition of a method nor by the nostalgic recollection of the happy practices of the olden times. A method is not an instrument that can be indifferently used as if the expression of a hegemonic subject, an emergent truth, or a triumphant historicity. This is why today we don't believe those who, in the midst of the current weakening of the will and the unquestionable diminishing of collective memory, feign a kind of virginity or an adolescent critique, as if a juvenile acne had erupted on their face where a beard already grows, and who fantasize about happy times of endless innovation within the linear rhythm of knowledge and its infinite openings. Faced with this, we can be sure of one thing. We have been beaten, that our defeat has an ontological gravity as important as the wealth of needs, desires and intelligence that resulted from the transformations of collective conscience and revolutionary action.

So our question is: does the import of this defeat cancel the import of the transformation? I don't know. In any case, let's have a look. We have suffered defeat. We must acknowledge this. We have to convince ourselves that it is impossible to recall or re-enact events. Even if there was a solution to all this, it would certainly not be Ulysses returning to Ithaca, or Abraham stepping into the unknown. This defeat represents a staunch limit, an obstacle that only an enormous critical ability will be able to remove from the path to knowledge and social subversion. We are left to reflect on this defeat, its causes, and on where the enemy defeated us, always remembering that memory isn't linear, and that there only is ethical survival. Today we face industrial modernization, the rediscovery of profit, the reinvention of the market – *"Dura lex sed lex"* [However harsh, it is the law]. We were defeated. The culture and struggles of the sixties were defeated in the seventies. The eighties saw a consolidation of the victory of capitalism. I am probably just an archaeological remain; the defeat was more important than the transformation we experienced, as everything seems to indicate that no space is spared by modernization at present. Our defeat was the primary goal of the enemy. It was the formal cause of their modernization. But today, what can link our negativity to their affirmation? The fact that modernization is only the replay and the powerful mystification of what we were, of the knowledge that we had. To mention a few examples: first, in the factory. Negatively, the blocking of the chain of command that we constituted had to be done away with, as did the demands for a minimal wage we had imposed through the progression of effective demand and in response to desires that could no longer be contained. Always in the factories, but positively coming from the bosses, a new hierarchy of production had to be established which rewarded those who accepted command with lighter workloads. Automation is freely invented as part of the very knowledge that comes with the refusal to work, but at present it is used on the contrary as a means of breaking and masking the general character of this proletarian need.

Secondly, within society, thanks to the perceptive, organized and intelligent wielding of public funds, we were in the process of organizing a new model for the social working day. In order to modernize, they had to beat us on this social level through inflation, through the reassertion and exasperation of repressive, hierarchical, and functional rules of exclusion, but at the same time, they had to give in to the whole process of tertiarization and the socialization of the entrepreneurs' capacities, which forced them to implement generalized and computerized control. A battle for power is currently developing in this field and is nowhere near settled. The computerization of the social is freely invented within the positive worker and proletarian utopia of a time of the working day freed from the boss command, and here it finds itself at present proven in the context of workers' cooperation, and applied against this cooperation to break the pressure of this need and exploit in a capitalist manner the power of socialized work (of work which has freed itself from a parasitic industrial territorialization and is revealed as social universality).

Finally, wherever the struggles and the desires for liberation manifested themselves, we have witnessed an always-identical mechanism: the repression of our power and the mystification of our knowledge, a ferocious and vile dialectic that crushed us. However, this dialectical enemy from within doesn't imply that today, when the time comes, we should forget the defeat that we suffered. On the contrary, it implies that we appreciate it in all its intensity. It certainly doesn't imply re-enacting impossible times past but rather confronting this new totality, this new machine of domination. This totality never ceases to be a tool for the enemy, it reclassifies the elements that concrete history provides it with and restructures them within the functional circularity of command. We own important, sometimes fundamental, segments that the machine of domination is currently reorganizing within a new totality. Our memory may well then linger over some of these segments; but this leaves our knowledge, in the midst of defeat, devoid of all strength. It can't find its bearings within the powerful mystified world offered to us, within this scene of things and command. In order to start living again and organize knowledge we must break this totality. To give fresh power to our segments, we must withdraw our being-segment from the totality in which it is imprisoned. Unless we destroy the totality to which we have been forced to comply, no proclamation of our contingent character and particularity will suffice, as it has done in the past, to rebuild the world. The destruction of this constraint of the totality is thus one of the first steps social practice should take; this, rather than paying respects to the memory of times past, or indulging in some nostalgia for the convulsions of anarchism or the professionalism of Jesuit bolshevism, or even participating in the Dionysian rhythm that, by attacking the heart of the state, at once destroys and lays claim to it! Because this destruction is the only way of freeing ourselves from the totality and of becoming free as a segment, as a particularity. A positive social practice can be built on this act of destructive freedom today. Reformism, revisionism, socialism, in short all the ways to name what, in the real movement, is opposed to communism, well, all of these are busy working to break the link between liberation and destruction! Be it social-democratic spinelessness, innovation on the continuity of values, or the Stalinist terrorism of the bureaucratic reduction of liberation to emancipation, in each case that link is negated.

Should it not then be noted how the concept of the left becomes blunt and meaningless when one of its fundamental and constitutive elements, precisely the link between liberation and destruction, is cast aside? The concept of the left is a concept for war. How can its destructive aspect be forgotten? How could the struggle for power reigning over the will for liberation be denied? Even more paradoxical is the fact that the great growth of our ability to understand power, its extensions, as described by Foucault, and its molecular penetration, as described by our dearest friends and comrades, is now held against us and used against us. As if the realization of complexity, instead of enabling us to carry out destruction more effectively, was in fact a labyrinth from which we can no longer escape. Why should-n't the power to master complexity be given to the knowledge of transformation? And be deployed with love for the singularities that constitute it, and against necessity, which on the contrary belongs to the enemy and the forces of conservation, the forces synonymous with the destruction of every single reason for life and freedom! There is a sort of ontological suspicion, not to say a real ethical allergy towards the idea of destruction, even amongst our closest comrades. One should in fact conceive of communism as an augmentation of being, and had we not been convinced of this all long, feminism would eventually have made it definitively obvious. But these resistances are unwarranted because the destruction that communist liberation requires doesn't reduce the surface of being. In this respect, I like to think of our destruction as performing a function comparable to that of philosophical doubt in the history of philosophy. In fact, doubt never insults, but always uncovers the horizon of being. Doubt, in all its forms, from Socratic ignorance to Cartesian doubt. But what destructive force can it introduce in the struggles for critical transformation? Let us consider Cartesian doubt. In the world of the sixteenth century, which saw the rise of the bourgeoisie and the birth of the modern state, a time when ideas had a reality and traditions had power, when magic still constituted a central frame of reference, doubt is not only a science that concerns ideas, but most of all one that has an effect on their concrete character, on their mechanical existence and material substance. Doubt is a destructive social practice that destroys things, not only fantasies and fictitious ideas. It is destructive in so far as it affirms freedom; it isn't a suspension of reality but a power against the mystified figure of the real, against the preponderance of power and illusions. The faith, mistake, falsehood of the ethical existence of truth can only exist thanks to the destruction of the prison of knowledge. Thus, power comes before knowledge. This is always the case. In the case of the boss, who, in order to dominate us, takes knowledge away from us and must also ground his dignity on power. Power is for him a material condition for knowledge. But equally, on our part, power is a condition of knowledge, a formal, not a material condition but nonetheless a very effective one.

Every time knowledge is taken away from us, it is because power has been taken away from us. It is true that our relation to knowledge via power is no vulgar matter. It doesn't possess the arbitrariness and blindness of anticipation, much less the continual overdetermination of knowledge. This, however, is the character and nature of the relation of the boss to being, as the law of value disappears and with it the progressive role of capital. Within transformative theory, the relationship between knowledge and power is the rich and productive link between destruction and liberation in transformative social practice. As regards the opposition between rational and irrational, I'd like to play with words by saying that, in such a metaphor, the capitalist anticipation of power over knowledge is irrational. The proletarian relation to it is on the contrary rational. By rational, here I mean a form that produces its own content. From a proletarian perspective, power and knowledge, destruction and liberation formally imply and feed one another. The current formal character of knowledge is the condition for the material anticipation of power in proletarian action. Knowledge thus legitimizes and power makes it just.

Let us now go back, my dear Félix, to determining our enquiry on social practice. To start the analysis over, let us outline a few premises. First of all, if destruction or the act of destroying is the internal condition of liberation, if this dynamic is fundamental to transformative theory, this isn't a reason for thinking that the processes of social practice consist in a simple flow. On the contrary, we cannot consider social practice as other than social agency and its investments, i.e. social tasks. So on the one hand, this is entirely ontological, which neither implies nor retains the possibility of superstructures or overdeterminations. On the other hand, this ontological condition is a network of structural divisions and of dimensions that are always territorialized in a specific fashion. Specification is manifested under the guise of the historical series of development of the forms and shapes taken on by social organization. What then does specification mean within this framework, how to determine the link between destruction and freedom, between knowledge and power? How does this relation manifest itself when we go from a very general discourse to the concrete dimension of our society, to the finite horizon of our ontological field, and we confront the machinic and deterritorialized substance of institutions and of state, collective and capitalist repressive structures? There are two ways to address this problem. The first is the structural organization of the state, which I will take here as an example. The second is the specific way to organize a process of liberation. In each of these perspectives, the question lies in the proliferation of meanings with which to define the complexity of social segments, the ontological and material functions that, by converging, form a synchronic network, accumulate through history, and gradually come to form a structural totality.

It is obvious, as you say, Félix, that when dealing with the state one is dealing with a complex and stratified ontological dimension comprising of a number of internal levels, each of which, in turn, is made available to the territorialization of command. These segments not only constitute the state, but they produce and reproduce themselves within subjectivity itself. So it is highly problematic to speak about the withering away of the state and absolutely absurd to evoke anything beyond a metaphor of its destruction pure and simple. It will still be possible to conceive of a new composition of the social segments of the state, an open composition with more deterritorialized phyla, thus breaking with capitalist policies of reterritorialization. All this however presupposes the permanence and substance of a historical accumulation of ontological experiences. If we return to the question, now from the perspective of the composition of society and of social subjects, we understand how running parallel to the process we described at the level of the state level there are similar processes at work. I mean to say that if within the state and the stratification of its structure, we can read the difficult development of the experiences of organization of society and the accumulation of the "means" intended to organize social labor, similarly, in the consciousness of social subjects and within their mass behavior, we discover elements of consistency and composition: experiences of struggle, defeat and victory, experiences of liberation and organization, but most of all the history and the phylum of this knowledge of liberation that this ample development has nourished.

There was a time when Italian and European workerists spoke of a technical and political composition of social classes. The double sided nature of this approach was purely methodological: the definitions were in fact absolutely homogeneous and their articulations had to find their verification in lived experience, and rightly so. Nonetheless, it is important to underline the convergence, noticeable today, between the methods of workerism and those of the most sophisticated forms of socio-historical enquiry. In following the historical series of development of the organization of the working day, the labor market, the structure of production and reproduction, and most of all the series of the cycles of struggle, workerism managed to develop what I still consider to be an unsurpassed and unsurpassable description of the evolution of the forms of class consciousness. The results of this old research now see their confirmation. The same applies to the history of the party, i.e. the history of the continuous dialectic of class consciousness between institutional "structure" and revolutionary "agency" – the history of the party, from anarchism to social democracy, from socialism to Leninism, finds itself explained by the linear evolution of class composition. Let it be clear that a process of accumulation is actually revealed through this evolution, a subjective movement of categorization, selection, and constitution. What was retained from past consciousness and experiences of organization served as a critical material means to formulate an ever renewed project of liberation. From this perspective, Leninism indeed subsumed anarchism and social democracy (which are its immediate precursors and adversaries) by reducing them to segments of a new organizational form, by recuperating them and reclassifying them within the original "agency" that it constituted. In the same way, today, inasmuch as liberation struggles can gain maturity and reach a decisive threshold, it is obvious that in these, the worker of automation and socialized information would understand and would subsume Leninism under a new form of social organization and of the struggle for liberation. Leninism competes with liberation, just as anarchism competes with Leninism. From this new perspective on struggle and organizing, Leninism is no doubt an element to be subsumed, even if it will always be kept alive in the agency that we are preparing.

Thus, we can go back to discussing the relationship between liberation and destruction. At the level of current social practices, in what can the moment of destruction consist of? It must consist of the destructuration of the totality within which segments of social and productive life, as well as proletarian knowledge, have been reorganized into a state since the defeat of the seventies. To unmake so-called modernization doesn't entail denying the importance of the technical and the material shifts through which it was realized. The question is rather to take them away and free them from the totality, to enable them to be disengaged from the ends that capitalism wishes to impose on them today, and therefore to move against the ordered reterritorialization that capitalism wants to coerce them into. To destroy means to initiate a process of general dislocation of all the elements of production and reproduction.

No doubt Leninism cannot be the fundamental drive behind a social process of such dimensions and at such levels. Since its origins, Leninism has been lacking the required dimensions and characteristics; as regards its extraneousness to the needs of a productive social class, shaped by a hegemonic conscience, it can even be largely criticized. But criticizing Leninism in this way doesn't mean treating it like dead dog – because it lives and will always live, like a stark reminder of the unforgettable function of class war (which cannot be erased or neglected), as an indication of the necessity to destroy the totality of the *dispositif* of command of the enemy – a never-ending task for those in search of liberation. The dislocation of the frame of liberation as a whole thus implies – as a critical moment – the destruction of the totality.

At this point, we open up to a new series of thoughts. Let us first repeat ourselves. Today we live in the age of defeat, let us never forget that. There is very little room for alternative social practice (a fact that, by itself, feeds the thought of destruction). Indeed, alternative social practice often tends to be realized within the general scheme of totality that produces power. Nonetheless, paradoxically, power is highly aware of the fact that within the scheme of totality it is holding and partitioning a knowledge that is not his but someone else's (a knowledge not predisposed towards mediation, harsh and often irreconcilable). It is true that the precariousness of domination is revealed less by the resistance of the oppressed than by the fragility of the relations of domination (in this respect it would be useful to analyze several dimensions: first the circulation and speed of consensus producing mechanisms, then the temporal dimension of legitimacy ... but we will talk about this some other time). This objective aspect of the crisis must not be underestimated. The level of synthesis achieved by domination and the capacity of the enemy to produce subjectivity are minimal, objectively minimal. The enemy totality hasn't managed to be (or to make itself) organic. However – and here come the new thoughts I mentioned – this isn't enough to set up a theory and social practice that include a new notion of "the left", that is to say it isn't enough to start thinking about theory and social practice as basic activities, as attempts at destroying the opposed totality, or as interventions in the objective contradictions – in short, social practice must not be just (a form of) thought of crisis. On the contrary, it should equally touch on the ontological dimension and develop the constitutive tendency. At present, the moment we destroy the ability of the enemy's totality to recuperate the knowledge of the exploited, we will have conquered the possibility of expressing the powerful fragmentation of theory, the deep irreducibility of desires, all the transversal tissues of agency. The future of our social practice lies in the destruction of the enemy totality as totality – not because this act of rupture is ontologically prevalent in the logic of social action, but simply because it opens up a great number of possibilities for expression. Social practice unveils itself as being the liberation of desiring segments. And when those expressions fully unfold, the war machines capable of destroying the totality can turn this destruction into a new beginning. The concept of a party and of "the left" cannot be defined here as the plenitude of expression of these segments and positive behaviors beyond the war machine.

At present we are faced with a set of historical experiences that seem to have an extreme novelty about them. These are Solidarnosc in Poland, the development of the Greens movement in West Germany, and a number of other new social movements, very large by comparison, although much less organized and still in need of critical analysis, such as the movement of the "self-convoked" in Italy, the struggle against NATO in Spain, the English miners' struggle, etc. These movements of organization and struggle have completely new characteristics when compared to traditional workers' organizations. Thus they can't be referred back to our memories and traditions. These movements display the ontological experience of the breaking of the totality and the liberation of an energy permanently directed against it. Defining the material foundations of the political composition of the exploited class by an analysis of this composition would not be difficult, but it isn't important for the moment. What matters is to insist on the extraordinary innovation present here. All the movements mentioned above were born after the great flood; it is worth remarking that not only the world still exists after the flood, but also that in fact this disaster has really fertilized the soil.

Let us examine the initial character of these movements.

First and foremost, they are social movements; secondly, they aren't reformist but different movements. Therefore, they are 1. transversal movements, 2. alternative movements. They don't want the totality, on the contrary they want to destroy it, and it is through this destruction that they assert the independence of their knowledge (its richness and rainbow multiplicity, etc.) and the efficiency of their power. I don't know the laws that enable these movements to make their presence a continued one – if these laws exist, they are yet to be discovered. But I would like to suggest a hypothesis. The passage from flow to substance, from movement to party, essentially depends on the ability of the physical strength of the masses and of radical intellectuals to establish a link between the power of new knowledge and the capacity for destruction. I feel that the degree of substance and organizational stability of ontological irreversibility of can only be measured and definitively established when the movement of struggle acknowledges itself as a machine geared to the radical displacement of the terms of politics. For the first time, the autonomy of the political is paradoxically brought about through the independence of the social as a refusal of the state (but only as the end of a utopian process which had been unfolding for too long).

Both the right and modern Liberalism understood a large number of the current characters of revolutionary knowledge: hence they tried to mystify them – and this is why we were treated to an orgy of *"nouveaux philosophes"*. No, to tell the truth, the independence of alternative politics has nothing to do with a resurgence of liberalism; what we want is a total socialization of the means of production, this seems obvious to us, even banal. However, this is not where the problem lies. The problem is a different one, and absolutely crucial. Freedom consists in positing an essential diversity in a world where all the possible conditions of freedom and truth have otherwise vanished, absorbed into the totality of power. Only the irruption of the other, of an ontological alternative into the sphere of institutional politics can give liberation a new meaning and thus establish a transformative social practice. Within the philosophies of knowledge and those of science, within aesthetics and all structural-functional systems, the emergence of the catastrophic element and of radical difference constitutes a fundamental moment precisely as man's perspective has been overshadowed by totality. Only a subversive use of the political is able to produce this overabundance of truth, to express an image of totality that wasn't closed, that was one of radical innovation, and thus managed to anticipate and point towards the concept of catastrophe: 1848, 1870, 1917, 1968 ... Without these catastrophes science would have never discovered thermodynamics... But now the problem is how to construct the catastrophe. This is to mention all of the enormous problems that we are unable to solve. However, there is one problem that we must solve: how to be the catastrophe by building it, how to be the totality without being it, how to be the destructive opposite of the capitalist and state totality without becoming homologous to it. Subversion as radical democracy, wherever the forms of organization have the efficiency of Leninism and the freedom of autonomism; social practice as an agency of singularities – without falling into fetishism, either of the "general will" or the "common good", both of which amount to a denial of difference and its treatment as a mere cog within the cosmos of exploitation.

To conclude: well, my dear Félix, what comes to mind is a terribly efficient and terribly adversary social practice, one that I've had to endure and that contributed to our defeat; namely, terrorism. It isn't very hard to define; what it is, is a monstrous event, a mystified rendition of state violence and of its empty fiction of totality, it is a mystical unilateral blitz that through destruction negates liberation by taking its dynamic force away from it and doing away with all the gentleness of its relations. However, terrorism is and has been deemed scandalous and will continue to be so unless we avoid the monstrous reproach it throws at us: that we haven't managed to become men who rebel without a fuss, who reclaim freedom and effect a rupture with an existence controlled by power. Terrorism could reproach us for not being free, for being, in the face of Goliath, sheep instead of Davids. We can only invent a new life, free from both terrorism and state violence, if we return to a form of militancy capable of putting forward the question of alternative values and of totally radical methods. As if our social practice was guided by the hypothesis of the existence of a few millions Davids.

"Power", if you wish, comes before "knowledge". Some will say, my dear Félix, that we are almost fascists when we say things like this. Let people talk. For my part, I would like to make things even worse, to show off bad taste and tawdriness: to say that love, only love, can determine the relation between power and knowledge. Some old friends are with me on this, and consider this shameful admittance of irrationalism legitimate. The first of these is the good Spinoza, who takes up the motto of the great philosophers of the Italian Renaissance and states that love is halfway between knowledge and power. And most of all, the eternal and Goethe-like Lenin: "at the beginning was action". Let us make haste.

Forthcoming

The Occupation Cookbook

Go. Create. Resist

Punkademics
Edited by Zack Furness

Spectacular Capitalism: Guy Debord and the Practice of Radical Philosophy
Richard Gilman-Opalsky

Art, Refusal and Multitude: Remapping the History of the Radical Avant-Garde
Edited by Gavin Grindon

Communization and its Discontents: Contestation, Critique, and Contemporary Struggles
Edited by Benjamin Noys

you can find them at yr local undercommons...

...or better yet,

create your own....
www.minorcompositions.info

Milton Keynes UK
Ingram Content Group UK Ltd.
UKHW022331100424
440921UK00001B/70